> YOUR MOTHERLAND
> IS AN ALTAR,
> NOT A PEDESTAL.
>
> JOSÉ MARTÍ

©2024 CATHERINE FET · NORTH LANDING BOOKS · ALL RIGHTS RESERVED

Toussaint Louverture
1743 – 1803

In 1804, the French colony of Saint-Domingue, populated by half a million African slaves and French plantation owners, became the world's first black republic. The name Saint-Domingue was replaced with Haiti – a Taíno Indian word meaning "mountainous land." The white band was ripped from the French tricolor and discarded. The Haitian flag – blue and red – was raised, to mark the victory of the 'slave revolution.' Remaining the only successful slave rebellion in history, the Haitian Revolution was led by a former slave, Toussaint Louverture, the 'Father of Haiti.'

At the end of the 18th century Saint-Domingue – the French portion of the island of Hispaniola, was the 'jewel' of the French colonial empire, its most profitable colony. It had 7,000 plantations producing sugar, indigo dye, coffee, cotton, and cocoa. It supplied French industry with cheap raw materials, keeping huge numbers of French workers employed. Every year plantation owners purchased up to 40 thousand Africans brought to Saint-Domingue by slave traders. Among them was a captured West African chieftain, the grandfather of Toussaint Louverture. Over the years French settlers intermarried with the Africans, forming an ethnic group known as the *Creoles* – people of mixed race. Toussaint Louverture was one of them. As a kid, Toussaint spoke *Creole French* – a mix of French and native African languages. Later he was taught standard French by Catholic Jesuit missionaries. It's likely that he also learned from them about the anti-slavery ideas of the French Enlightenment thinkers, such as the Jesuit French abolitionist Abbé Raynal. However, in 1763 the Jesuits were expelled from Saint-Domingue for spreading Christianity among the slaves. This activity clashed with French plantation owners' belief that slaves didn't have the brain power to grasp the ideas of Christian faith. Toussaint Louverture didn't learn to write until he was in his mid-40s.

L'ouverture, tous saints

*Toussaint Louverture's last name was either a nickname or an 'inspirational' name he adopted. In French, **l'ouverture** is "the opening, the beginning." It's possible that it referred to breaking the enemy defenses in a battle. 'Toussaint' comes from the French **tous saints** – "all saints" (La Toussaint = All Saints Day)*

Haitian Revolution flag "Liberty or Death" (French)

The *Code Noir* – 'The Black Law' – signed by French King Louis XIV, mandated that all slaves in French colonies had to convert to Catholicism and take French names, but plantation owners felt that Christian ideas, such as equality of people before God, could provoke slaves to rebel. Africans brought with them their native customs and beliefs – worship of animal and plant spirits and rituals of traditional magic. These beliefs seemed scary to the French but they put up with them. So, in the Caribbean these elements of native faith blended with Christianity, creating a new religion, *Voodoo* (or 'vodou'). Voodoo priests had a lot of authority in slave communities, and some of them were familiar with the ideas of abolitionism.

Slaves in Saint-Domingue had no rights. For any misstep they were whipped, and at any suspicion of rebellion put in chains and branded – like criminals were – with the French *fleur-de-lis*.

The Fleur-de-lis

The Fleur-de-lis, or the 'lily flower,' was a medieval heraldic symbol in the shape of a lily. It appeared on the coat of arms of the French kings and became the symbol of the French monarchy.

"Slaves cutting the sugar cane" and "Slaves' stick fight" – vintage prints

Creole

The word *Creole* (*Créole* in French) comes from the Portuguese verb 'criar' – 'to raise a child' (same root as English 'create' – from the Latin 'creare'). In Portuguese, 'crioulo' referred to a person raised in someone's house together with their own children. In Spanish-speaking countries the word Criollo described the descendants of Europeans born in the Americas. In the Caribbean, however, it was mostly used to refer to mixed-race people.

However the life of Saint-Domingue slaves was not entirely hopeless. Those who were capable of more than *manual labor* could help plantation managers overseeing the work and even be *manumitted* – released from slavery. As a matter of fact, most plantations were run by former slaves or creole *freemen*, since most of the actual plantation owners, the *grands blancs*, lived in France. The manager of the Breda plantation where Louverture's family were slaves, Bayon de Libertad, was impressed with Toussaint's abilities and allowed him unlimited access to his home library. He eventually freed Louverture. Years later, during the anti-slavery uprising, Louverture saved Bayon de Libertad from angry rebels by hiding him and his family in the woods and secretly bringing them food. He then helped Bayon de Libertad's family escape to the United States and supported them financially for years.

The Grands and Petits Blancs

*In Haiti, poor white settlers who didn't own plantations were called **petits blancs** – the 'little whites.' Those who were wealthy and owned plantations were the **grands blancs** – the 'big whites.'*

Manual Labor and Manumission

***Manual labor** literally means 'work done with one's hands' and refers to 'physical' labor – work that requires physical effort and very little training. 'Manual' comes from the Latin word **manus** – hand. The same Latin word appears in **manumission** – the ritual of granting freedom to a slave. In Ancient Rome 'manus' was also a legal term – 'master's hand,' or 'the power of a master.' So Latin 'manū mittere' meant 'to let go of the master's control.'*

The island of Hispaniola – French Saint-Domingue and Spanish Santo Domingo

"Shipping out sugar on Sainte-Domingue"

Once free, Toussaint Louverture worked for Bayon de Libertad on a salary and saved up enough money to rent a small plantation with 13 slaves. One of these slaves was Jean-Jacques Dessalines, Louverture's comrade-in-arms and the future first ruler of liberated Haiti. Louverture got married and 'purchased' his wife, Cécile, and her family from their plantation owner – to set them free. Cécile and Louverture had two kids, but his plantation business didn't go well in the beginning, and Cécile abandoned him for a wealthy Creole plantation owner. Eventually Toussaint Louverture bought several coffee plantations, becoming a wealthy planter and slave owner himself. Enslaving defeated tribes was a common practice in Africa. Most enslaved Africans brought to the European colonies were captured and sold to European slave traders by African leaders who had won a tribal war. So, while most enslaved Africans recognized the cruel nature of slavery, seeing slavery as a criminal practice wasn't common.

As the French Revolution broke out in 1789, a couple Creole merchants whose fathers were white asked the new French revolutionary government, the French National Assembly, to give to *gens de couleur* – free 'people of color' – the same rights as were enjoyed by the white French settlers. Turned down, they returned to Saint-Domingue and started an uprising. Even though the uprising failed and its leaders were executed, the unrest continued and spread to other Caribbean islands. Toussaint Louverture, however, at that point identified as a French royalist. He wore a white royalist cockade on his sleeve and didn't support the rebels' quest for more rights.

"Battle for Palm Tree Hill" (the Haitian Revolution) by January Suchodolski

As the unrest continued, the French revolutionary government finally agreed to grant French citizenship to free people of color. But it was 'too little, too late,' and did not stop the rebellion. The black and mixed-race slaves, realizing that they could be French citizens if they were free, demanded the abolition of slavery.

15 sols silver coin, colonial Saint-Domingue

A Jamaican Voodoo priest named Dutty "Zamba" Boukman organized a Voodoo ceremony, calling on the spirits of his people's African ancestors to destroy the French slave owners. As the ceremony was held, a tropical storm arrived. Its intense thunder and lightning were interpreted by the ceremony participants as a sign. Many rushed to their plantations and started killing white plantation managers and owners. This event unified African slaves, Creole slaves, and freemen. Toussaint Louverture was present at the ceremony and within weeks he led the rebel armies against the *militias* of the French settlers in a war that would continue for 12 years.

Initially Toussaint Louverture's ability to control his forces was very limited. The slave rebels were unruly. As they swept over the island, plantation homes were burned and whites were killed – all, grownups, women, and children, as well as their African servants. Heads of white kids were put on pikes and carried as banners by the rebel mobs. French historian Louis Dubroca in his book *The Life of Toussaint Louverture* (published in 1802) paints a picture of extreme violence – massacres and tortures performed by the rebels, displaying "a fanaticism that murders without remorse in the name of heaven, and an extreme barbarism for which the sacred laws of nature and humanity have no restraint."

Militia

Militia is a military force made of armed civilians – not military men. Both 'militia' and 'military' come from the Latin **mīles** (plural **mīlitēs**) – soldier.

Dutty Boukman's Voodoo Ceremony in Bois-Caiman (Ogier Fombrun Museum, Haiti)

In a memoir *Reminiscences of the Insurrection in Saint Domingo*, American merchant Samuel G. Perkins, who happened to be in Saint-Domingue during the uprising, tells a story of a white planter's family whose carriage was stopped by the rebels: "The plantations were in flames on all sides of them, and the hands of the slaves were still wet with the blood of their former owners...The first step of the insurgents [rebels], after stopping the carriage, was to pull out of it a black nanny and a white child. 'Take him into the field,' said one of the savages, 'and cut off his head!' But the child's grandmother exclaimed, 'Stop, wretch! have you no children of your own? What has he done to your race that you should destroy him? If you wish for blood and for vengeance on one who has held you in bondage, take my life!' Then she addressed the women in the crowd, 'How can you allow them to commit this horrible crime? I see tears of compassion in your eyes... Go and save the child, and save your own soul!' A shout arose among the women of the insurgents, they ran to the spot where the child had been carried and brought him back." One of Louverture's 19th-century biographers, C.W. Eliott, pointed out that Louverture was known for seeking to curb violence,"Shocked at the cruelties of whites and blacks, he took the side of mercy and saved lives from the sword as well as from disease." (*Saint Domingo, Its Revolution, and Its Hero Toussaint Louverture*, 1855)

In the early stage of the 'slave revolution' Louverture sided with the Spanish against the French revolutionaries, but in 1794 the French revolutionary government proclaimed the abolition of slavery, and Louverture changed sides. Now he was fighting against the Spanish and against many of his own rebel friends who were still on the Spanish side. Plus, he organized guerilla warfare against British troops who had also landed on Saint-Domingue hoping to take advantage of the civil war and capture the island for the English crown.

Guerilla

*Guerillas (from Spanish **guerra** – war) are civilians who fight against an enemy army in small independent groups, using 'guerilla tactics,' such as disrupting enemy supplies, burning warehouses with enemy ammunition, capturing enemy messengers, and so on.*

Toussaint Louverture's military success brought him fame and admiration across the Caribbean and in France. They called him the Black Spartacus in reference to the famous leader of the slave uprising in Ancient Rome.

Louverture was also respected for his loyalty to the Christian faith. He never fell for the anti-religious propaganda of the Enlightenment intellectuals and the French revolutionaries. One of Toussaint's Spanish supporters, Marquis d'Hermona wrote about him, "If an angel were to descend upon earth, he could not inhabit a heart kinder than that of Toussaint Louverture." Quoting him, Louis Dubroca, a passionate critic of Louverture, adds, "All Toussaint's actions are covered with such a profound veil of hypocrisy, that, although his entire life has been a series of treachery and crimes, all who approach him are betrayed into an opinion of the purity of his intentions." Describing Louverture, Dubroca provides these details: "This celebrated Negro is of the middle stature [height]. He has fine eyes, and his glances are rapid and penetrating. Extremely sober by habit, his activity in the prosecution of his enterprises [carrying out his plans] never stops...He sleeps generally in his clothes, and gives very little time either to sleep or his meals. His dress is usually a general's uniform. He always has a handkerchief twisted round his head, over which he wears a military hat. His disposition is dark and silent. He seldom speaks the French language, and if he does, he speaks poorly."

The French promoted Louverture to general and arranged for his sons, 11 and 14-years-old, to attend a school for the kids of colonial officials in France. So, in Paris, Louverture's sons were invited to dinners and parties with members of the French elite such as Joséphine de Beauharnais, wife of Napoleon Bonaparte and future Empress of France. It was a typical practice for colonial powers to offer such education to the children of their 'puppet' rulers in the colonies, but in the case of Louverture there was an additional – more sinister – reason. He scared the French government. So his sons were to be used as hostages if Louverture ever thought to rebel against the French. The Louverture kids, however, weren't easy to control either! They regularly escaped from school and had their own fun in wild, revolutionary Paris.

While most rebel leaders demanded death for the white settlers, Louverture focused on ideas of equality, not race. He said, "I am black, but I have the soul of a white man" to underline that his loyalty to France and his Catholic faith were above racial loyalty. This position contrasted sharply with that of many local leaders. One of them, Sonthonax, a white Saint-Domingue politician who married a free black woman, responded to Louverture with, "I am white, but I have the soul of a black man." Sonthonax opposed the return of the white settlers who had fled from Saint-Domingue. Louverture, on the contrary, saw them as successful entrepreneurs who could restore the economy of the colony ruined by the revolution.

Some white business people and settlers returned to Saint-Domingue based on Louverture's promise that they would be protected. Even his enemies admitted that "Toussaint never broke his word."

In his memoir Samuel Perkins describes Port au Prince before and during the revolution: [Before the revolution] "during the working days the blacks enlivened the scene by their rough but cheering songs as they pursued their labor, with constant explosions of loud laughter. On Sundays, groups of dancers took the place of laborers, and the drum and the pipe and the laugh and the song made the air ring with joy. Now all was hushed as death; not even the dip of an oar or the sight of a boat. The stores and warehouses that used to be loaded with merchandise from all parts of the world lay smoldering in flames, and the harbor that formerly was filled with the ships had only a few small vessels at its outer anchorage." Louverture was very concerned with the fact that the work of the plantations had stopped and the trade with France was disrupted. Thousands of people were plunged into extreme poverty. The other factor was Louverture's own plantation business. In the course of the revolution he purchased over 30 properties and was the richest man on the island. He wanted the plantation business to be back.

Meanwhile in France, their own revolution was dying. There were rumors that the new government led by Napoleon Bonaparte was planning to reestablish slavery to save the economy of the island. Both in Europe and in the United States, politicians were terrified that the success of the Saint-Domingue revolution would inspire slave uprisings not only in the Caribbean, but also in the South American colonies, and in the South of the United States. Another concern was the infighting between the revolutionaries in Saint-Domingue which resulted in a year-long civil war. Even though Louverture's side won, their reputation was destroyed by the cruel tactics of Louverture's lieutenant, Jean-Jacques Dessalines who slaughtered up to 10 thousand prisoners of war and civilians – all black and mixed-race islanders. In 1801 Louverture invaded the Spanish portion of Hispaniola. Soon controlling the entire island he called together a constitutional assembly. The group working on the constitution for Saint-Domingue was made mostly of white plantation owners.

Jean-Jacques Dessalines

The constitution made Louverture governor-general of the island for life. It also stated that slavery was "forever abolished. All men are born, live, and die free and French." However, bringing new slaves from Africa and forcing them to work on plantations was still permitted. In 1803 Louverture's biographer James Stephen praised the improvement of the island's economy under Louverture's rule: "This great and growing produce was obtained without the miseries of West India slavery. Men were obliged to work,

General Leclerc

but it was in a moderate manner, for fair wages; and they were for the most part at liberty to choose their own work. The plantation black workers were therefore in general contented, healthful, and happy." Stephen also pointed out that the numbers of newborn babies in Saint-Domingue sharply increased during the revolution and the infant mortality (baby death) fell. He attributed it to the absence of slave labor. Another article of the Saint-Domingue constitution allowed only one religion in Saint-Domingue – Catholicism. This reflected Louverture's desire to distance himself from Voodoo and the African roots of the Saint-Domingue slaves. "He proclaims amnesty for all political offenders, and keeps it!" wrote C.W. Eliott. "He invites both whites and blacks to return to their work. He orders *Te Deum* to be sung in the churches, and orders that morning and evening prayers be read to troops. Of course his enemies say this is hypocrisy!"

In France, however, Napoleon suspected that sooner or later Louverture would declare

Te Deum

Te Deum laudamus ('You, God, we praise') is a 4th-century Latin Christian hymn.

Saint-Domingue independent from France. So he sent 20,000 French troops to Saint-Domingue to restore 'order.' "He was resolved to seize the seacoast by surprise and violence, but afterwards to subdue his enemies by bribery and cunning, rather than by war," wrote James Stephen in his book *Buonaparte in the West Indies, or, The history of Toussaint Louverture, the African hero*. Napoleon's brother-in-law, General Leclerc who commanded this expedition had secret orders to seize Louverture (whom Napoleon nicknamed the 'gilded African') and all black officers of his government and bring them to France.

The two sons of Toussaint Louverture who studied in France were on one of Leclerc's ships – to be used as hostages if necessary. Leclerc's forces landed in three spots on the island. At Fort Dauphin they marched onto the beach in a battle formation. Local people started gathering around chanting "No whites!" and were immediately slaughtered.

To defend Saint-Domingue Toussaint Louverture was planning to burn the coastal cities, retreat with his troops into the mountains, and let the yellow fever and starvation destroy Napoleon's forces. These plans were disrupted by Napoleon's idea to bribe Louverture's black generals. Two of them, including Jean-Jacques Dessalines, betrayed Louverture and switched sides in exchange for keeping their rank in the French military. For this betrayal Dessalines and his wife received lavish gifts from the French generals. Meanwhile, the French sent the two sons of Louverture accompanied by their tutor and a French military unit to Toussaint Louverture's house. Louverture and his wife hadn't seen the kids for 8 years. Using the emotional intensity of this moment, the tutor conveyed to Louverture Leclerc's offer to surrender on the condition that he would retain "respect, honors, and fortune," and be appointed the French Lieutenant-General of the island.

According to James Stephen, the tutor said, "Look at the tears of your wife, and consider, that upon your decision depends whether the boys shall remain to gladden her heart and yours, or be torn from you both forever." Next Louverture's son Isaac addressed his dad "with a speech which his tutor had no doubt assisted him in preparing. He described how kindly he was received by the Consul [Napoleon], and what high esteem and regard he expressed for Toussaint Louverture and his family. The younger brother added something which he had been taught to the same effect, and both tried to win their father to a purpose, of the true nature and consequences of which they had no idea."

"The blockade of Saint-Domingue by Leclerc" by Louis-Philippe Crépin

Just when the French thought Louverture was about to agree, he invited his kids' tutor to the next room and said, "Take back my children, since it must be so. I will be faithful to my brethren and my God."

Louverture's kids were taken back to France, and the French unleashed the war. After many battles Louverture's forces were retreating. One of the French generals, Brunet, invited Louverture to his house for negotiations. "You will find nothing here but the frankness of an honorable man who desires only your happiness for the colony," promised Brunet. Toussaint agreed to come and arrived with a few guards. "Brunet and his companions are charming," wrote C.W. Eliott, "They talk about the troops, they go over the maps... The evening comes... Brunet leaves the room. Colonel Ferrari enters it with twenty men, their swords drawn. He says: 'I have orders to arrest you. If you resist, you are a dead man. Give me your sword.'" In June, 1802 Louverture was taken to France along with over a 100 members of his family and supporters. Boarding the ship, captive Toussaint Louverture addressed the French, "In overthrowing me you have cut down only the trunk of the tree of liberty. It will spring up again from the roots, for they are numerous and they are deep."

In a report to Napoleon Leclerc wrote about the arrested Louverture's supporters, "I have put some of them on board the frigate Mucron, which has orders to proceed to the Mediterranean..." This was likely the reference to the practice of selling prisoners of war into slavery to Muslim slave traders on the Barbary Coast. However, Napoleon's critics suspected that 'Mediterranean' was actually a code word for drowning prisoners, because most of them vanished with no evidence of their sale into slavery.

Napoleon thought of exhibiting Louverture in a cage on a square in Paris, but ended up keeping him imprisoned at a fortress in the Jura mountains of France. Louverture died 7 months later, in a prison, likely from pneumonia and malnutrition. Meanwhile, the following year, the Haitian revolution entered its most violent stage. Suffering massive casualties, defeated in battles, and losing thousands of soldiers to yellow fever, the French withdrew from Saint-Domingue, and Haiti established its independence. With Toussaint Louverture gone, Jean-Jacques Dessalines became the head of the Republic of Haiti and ordered the Haitian Genocide of 1804 – the massacre of all white people remaining in the country. Former slaves went door to door killing whole families. Mixed-race soldiers were also forced to participate in the killings so that the blame didn't fall exclusively on the Africans. Up to 5,000 were murdered.

The burning of Cap-Français, the most important port in Saint-Domingue, during an anti-colonial uprising in 1793

Simón Bolívar
1783 – 1830

Simón Bolívar is the South American hero who helped to free a number of countries from Spanish rule – Colombia (including today's Panama), Venezuela, Ecuador, Peru, and Bolivia. Even though his dream – to unite the Spanish colonies into the 'United States' of South America – didn't come true, his work and sacrifice forever changed that part of the world.

At the end of the 18th century Spain's grip on its colonies in South America was firm. Emigrating to the colonies or going there on business required the approval of the Spanish king. Any ship found in South American waters without license from Spain was attacked. Taxes were sky-high. Keeping stores, importing and exporting goods, and other forms of business activity were allowed only to people of Spanish descent. Native people could only do manual work. Planting vineyards or olive trees was forbidden – all wine and oil were imported from Spain. Building roads or developing local industries was discouraged. Printing books was impossible in most colonies – printing presses were neither built, nor imported. Spanish King Charles IV stated that learning wasn't "advisable" for America. To prevent revolutionary ideas from reaching the colonies, Spanish colonial authorities prohibited sale of books without their approval.

Racial and social divisions were encouraged by colonial authorities and used as tools of control. Native people – the 'Indians' – were supposed to hate the *Mestizos* (mixed-race Native-Spanish people), the *Mulattos* (mixed race African-Spanish people), and the *Pardos* (tri-racial, Native-African-Spanish people). All these groups – along with African slaves – were encouraged to hate the white Creoles. However, the political power in the colonies was not in the hands of the Creoles. Local governments were made of *Peninsulares* – colonists born in Spain ('from the peninsula' – the Iberian Peninsula, where Spain and Portugal are located.) So, on top of the racial split, there was rivalry and hatred between the Creoles and Peninsulares.

Simón Bolívar was a Creole, born in the city of Caracas, Venezuela, to a Creole family of Spanish nobility who came to South America in the 16th century. Bolívar's dad was a merchant, and one of the wealthiest men in South America. By the time Simón was 15, his parents died leaving their kids a large fortune. Simón Bolívar inherited 4 *haciendas* (plantations), two houses in Caracas, one in La Guaira, and large numbers of slaves. In 1799 Bolívar's uncle sent him to study in Madrid, Spain, where Simón fell in love with Maria Teresa Toro, daughter of a wealthy Creole businessman from Caracas who had moved to Spain. Bolívar was 17, Maria was 19. They were married 2 years later and immediately left for Venezuela. However, only 8 months after their arrival, Maria died of the dreaded yellow fever. Bolívar was devastated and vowed to never again be married. Writing about Maria's death, Spanish historian Salvador de Madariaga noted, "This sudden end of a 21-year-old girl has perhaps been one of the key events in the history of the New World."
This tragedy changed the course of Bolívar's life.

After Maria's death Bolívar sailed back to Madrid to bring his father-in-law the sad news. While in Europe, he reconnected with his old tutor, Simón Rodriguez who was in exile from Venezuela because of his ties to a pro-independence group of conspirators who attempted an uprising in 1797. Trying to distract Bolívar from his grief, Rodriguez did everything to channel his student's thoughts toward politics. They traveled to Paris, and to Italy just around the time Napoleon proclaimed himself emperor. In Milan they saw Napoleon crowned as King of Italy. Bolívar had been an admirer of Napoleon, but now he viewed him as a threat to freedom. In Rome, Bolívar and Rodriguez visited Mons Sacer (the 'Sacred Hill'). In 494 BC Roman *plebeians* (the common people), frustrated by poverty and debt, left Rome (ruled by *patricians* – the wealthy and privileged class) for Mons Sacer. They elected their own government, and refused to return. Inspired by this history of the Roman Republic and the sacrifices of the heroes who defended its sovereignty, Bolívar made a solemn vow to free the South American colonies from Spanish rule.

"Bolívar's wedding" by Tito Salas

Among Spanish colonies, Venezuela was one of the poorest. It didn't send gold and silver to Spain, like Mexico and Peru. Colonists and the native people were both robbed by impossibly-high taxes. So when Napoleon invaded Spain in 1807 and replaced the Spanish king Ferdinand VII with his brother Joseph, Venezuelan Creoles seized the opportunity to create their own government. On July 5, 1811 Venezuela declared its independence. Bolívar went on a diplomatic mission to Britain trying to gain British support for the Venezuelan government, but the mission failed, and eventually he joined the Venezuelan army fighting against the pro-Spanish Royalists.

At first the Republican army (supporters of the Republic of Venezuela) was successful, but in 1811 a powerful earthquake devastated Caracas. Many Venezuelans interpreted this event as God's punishment for declaring independence from Spain, and support for the republic collapsed. Bolívar was sent to defend Puerto Cabello, a port on the Caribbean Sea where most of the Republican army's ammunition was stored. But one of the officers of the fort's garrison sided with the Royalists. He armed Royalist prisoners kept in a Puerto Cabello jail and turned the fort cannons against the Republican army. Bolívar escaped and the Republican army surrendered to the Royalists. Soon, however, Bolívar appeared in New Granada, a Spanish colony that included territories of present-day Colombia, Ecuador, Panama, and Venezuela. From New Granada Bolívar led a force of independence fighters to retake Venezuela. He started out with only 500 men, but as battles were won, his army grew. On June 15, 1813, he published his controversial **Decree of War to the Death** ordering that any Spaniard who doesn't join the Republican army should be executed by a firing squad.

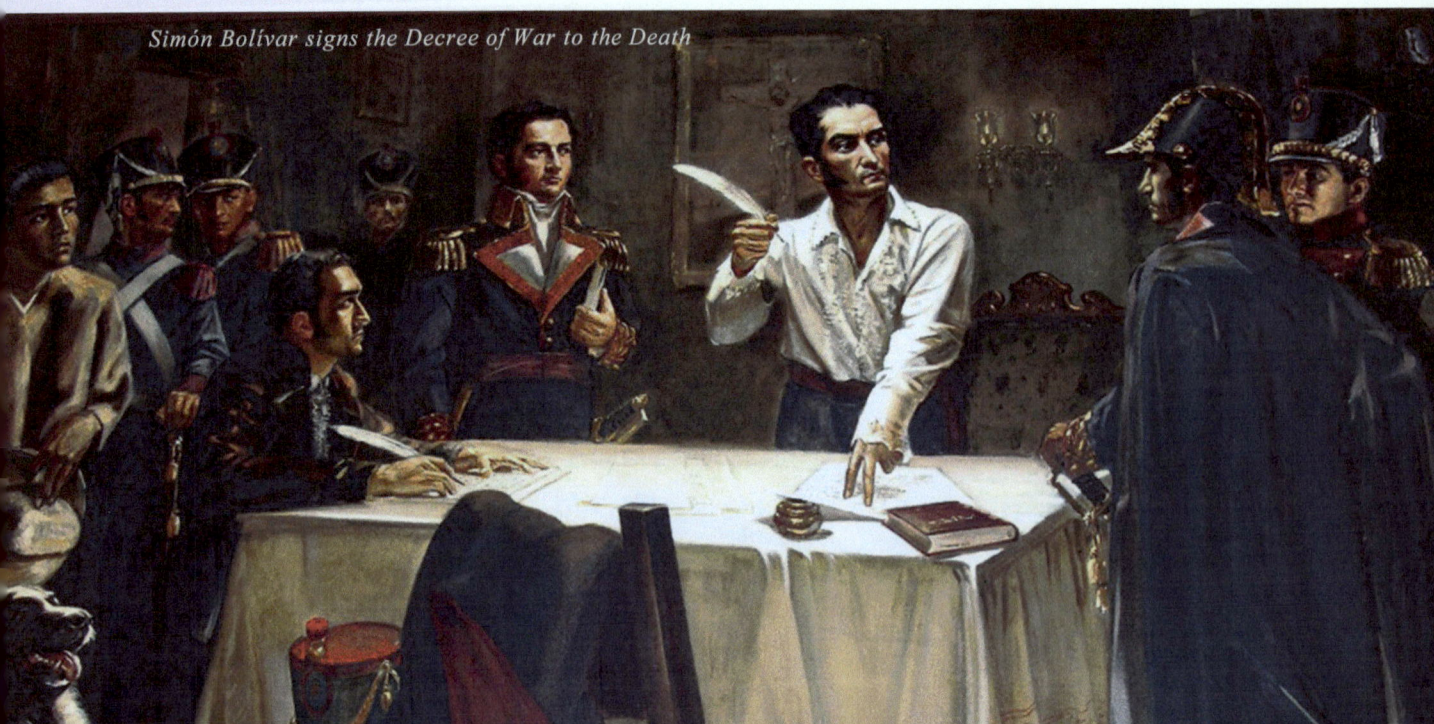

Simón Bolívar signs the Decree of War to the Death

Having defeated 5 Royalist armies in 6 battles, Bolívar entered Caracas on August 6. People in the streets cried and shouted, "Long live the Liberator! Long live the savior of Venezuela!" Young women, dressed in white brought crowns of laurel to Bolívar, church bells rang, and flowers covered his path. Bolívar was given the title of 'Liberator' and the powers of a dictator.

But the majority of Venezuelans were not sold on independence and resented the hardships of the war. So, a civil war broke out. The Venezuelan *llaneros*, the 'horsemen of the plains' (cowboys, cattle herders), led by *caudillo* (warlord) José Boves took the side of the Spanish and organized themselves into a powerful cavalry army. They also attracted African slaves and Pardos (tri-racial people) into their ranks, paying their soldiers with plunder. Boves' troops became known for extreme cruelty and violence, killing and torturing civilians, including kids, on any suspicion of being Republican sympathizers. Bolívar also felt that following the 'rules of war,' such as humane treatment of prisoners, was out of place when fighting an enemy who followed no rules. So when Boves' army approached Caracas, and the commander of La Guaira fortress asked Bolívar what to do with the Spanish prisoners kept there, Bolívar responded, "I order you to immediately execute all the Spaniards in the fortress and in the hospital, without exception." The same order was given in Caracas. 886 Spaniards and natives of the Canary Islands were executed. Bolívar also ordered his troops to seize all the gold and silver from the city treasuries and cathedrals. Caracas fell to the Royalists again, and Bolívar fled with 20,000 of his soldiers and civilians. Boves took over.

Following this defeat, independence fighters regrouped under a few caudillos – warlords – in various regions of the Spanish colonies. From that moment on, Bolívar's greatest challenge was to keep the caudillos from unleashing a civil war.

"Llaneros" by Celestino Martinez

Pursued by the Royalists, Bolívar sailed with the Caracas gold and silver treasure to Margarita Island. But the Republican officer in control of the island, Manuel Piar, declared Bolívar a traitor and sent him back to the mainland. There Bolívar lost the treasure and had to flee. Piar was a Pardo, suspicious of all white Creoles, especially Bolívar, who was, after all, a wealthy slave owner. Bolívar fled to New Granada, and from there sailed for Jamaica in May of 1815. While he stayed in Jamaica, the Spanish paid one of his former slaves (whom Bolívar had freed) to assassinate him. Bolívar escaped death because on the night of the assassination he let his secretary sleep in his hammock. The assassin stabbed the sleeping man with a dagger, thinking it was Bolívar.

From Jamaica Bolívar sailed to the Republic of Haiti. Haitian president, Alexander Pétion, promised to give Bolívar money and ammunition for a new expedition to the continent. In return he asked for only one thing: "When your expedition lands in Venezuela, free the slaves. For how can you run a republic where slavery exists?" Having landed in Venezuela, Bolívar freed his own slaves, and issued a proclamation granting freedom to the slaves who fought in his army. However, he fully supported the abolition of slavery only 10 years later. The reason for his hesitancy were his concerns about allowing racial equality. Since most independence fighters were white, and large numbers of them perished in the wars, Bolívar was afraid that the white colonists would lose power and the colonies would turn into 'pardocracia' (republics ruled by the 'people of color' – the Pardos' majority).
"In Venezuela, we have seen the free population die and the slaves survive," he wrote.

In 1815, Spain sent its biggest army ever to cross the Atlantic – to the American colonies. Its commander was Pablo Morillo. Napoleon had been defeated – first in Russia and then in Europe, and the Spanish King Fernando VII returned to the throne. He was eager to bring the rebellious colonies back under Spanish rule.

Pablo Morillo (top) and José Tomás Boves

Bolívar's expedition landed on Margarita Island and then made its way to the mainland, but despite many successes they couldn't defeat the Spanish. The infighting between Bolívar's caudillo 'generals' was a huge problem. Manuel Piar (the same guy who had once kicked Bolívar out of Margarita Island) claimed that Margarita Island and Guyana were 'his territories,' and rebelled. Bolívar dismissed him from the Republican army. Piar tried to raise his followers – mostly Pardos and Africans – against Bolívar, telling them he had been dismissed because he wasn't white. Bolívar ordered his arrest and public execution, "for proclaiming the odious principles of race war... for inciting civil war, and for encouraging anarchy." He wrote about Piar, "The death of General Piar was a political necessity which saved the country, for otherwise he would have started a war of Pardos against whites, leading to the extermination of the latter and the triumph of the Royalists."

In 1819 Bolívar finally found the road to success. He decided to leave Venezuela and first conquer New Granada. To achieve this he crossed the Andes mountains – in an area the Spanish considered impassable – and took the city of Bogotá. The Royalist troops lost the Battle of Boyacá and surrendered. This campaign by Simón Bolívar is still considered one of the most daring in military history. Here is how Bolívar's biographer Guillermo Sherwell describes the crossing of the Andes: "In the distance rose the snowy peaks of the eastern range of the Cordillera, and the waters of the plain through which they had waded were here replaced by the rapids and cataracts of mountain streams. The roads in many places followed the edge of steep precipices, and were bordered by gigantic trees, while the clouds above them poured down incessant rains..."

"Battle of Boyacá" by J. W. Cañarete

"...To cross the frequent torrents there were only narrow, trembling bridges formed of tree-trunks, or the 'aerial taravitas.' These consisted of ropes made by twisting several thongs of well-greased hides. The ropes were tied to trees on the two banks of the ravine, while from them was suspended a cradle or hammock of capacity for two persons, which was drawn backward and forward by long lines. Horses and mules were similarly drawn across, suspended by straps around their bodies."

On December 17, 1819, a new state, the Republic of Colombia was established. It included the territories of present-day Colombia, Panama, Venezuela, and Ecuador. The republic was mostly 'on paper' because a lot of these territories were still under Spanish control. The Spanish army led by General Morillo expected reinforcements from Spain. King Fernando VII was afraid of his own military which was 'infected' with liberal ideas, and was planning to get rid of the units led by liberally-minded officers by sending them to the colonies. But the army units selected for the colonial expedition started an uprising in Cadiz (Spain), demanded a constitution, and refused to fight for the King. The 'Cadiz Liberal Revolution' gave an impulse of renewed inspiration to the colonies' independence fighters. Bolívar reached out to General Morillo proposing a 6-month *armistice* (an agreement to stop fighting) and exchange of prisoners. Knowing that the reinforcements were not coming, Morillo agreed.

"We must conquer or die! And we will conquer, for Heaven does not want us in chains" – Simón Bolívar

After years of fighting Bolívar, General Morillo had a dream. He was dying to meet the enemy for whom he had developed tremendous respect. So one day Morillo invited Bolívar to get together, and they met on no-man's land, accompanied by a few officers. The two men were in many ways each other's opposites. Morillo was born in a poor family and climbed the ladder of a military career from the lowest rung to the highest. Bolívar was born in wealth, but sacrificed everything for his cause, gave away all his property, and shared the life of common soldiers. And yet, as a military man and a statesman, Bolívar had more in common with Morillo than with his own warlord generals. The two men embraced one another and had a drink together. Proposing a toast, Bolívar said, "To the heroic firmness of all the fighters of both armies... to their constancy, endurance and matchless bravery... to the worthy men who support and defend freedom in the face of ghastly losses...to those who have gloriously died defending their country and their government... to the wounded men of both armies who have shown their intrepidity, their dignity and their character... eternal hatred to those who desire blood and who shed it unjustly."

Morillo answered, "May Heaven punish those who are not inspired with the same feelings of peace and friendship that animate us." This meeting had a profound impact on Morillo. He realized that Spain would never win its war. Soon he asked the king to be recalled from the colonies, and left for Spain.

The decisive battle won by Bolívar in 1821 was the battle fought at Carabobo, a village in the high Andes, near the city of Valencia. A native guide who was helping Bolívar told him he knew a secret mountain footpath that could take Bolívar's men into the rear of the Spanish army. At night Bolívar's soldiers crossed the mountains and defeated the Spanish in a surprise attack, killing over 6000 Spaniards. The independence of Venezuela was secured.

Above: "Battle of Carabobo" by Martín Tovar y Tovar; Right: "The Spanish surrender at Carabobo" by Arturo Michelena

Bolívar was now a celebrity. Famous English poet Lord Byron (who later perished in the Greek War of Independence) named his yacht 'Bolívar' in his honor. In every town where Bolívar stopped there were celebrations and speeches praising the Liberator. Once, after a long march, Bolívar stopped at a small town where local authorities organized a reception in his honor. A town representative started reading a speech that seemed endless. When he came to the sentence "When Caesar crossed the Rubicon," Bolívar interrupted him. "My dear friend," he said, "when Caesar crossed the Rubicon, he had had his breakfast, and I haven't yet had mine. Can we eat first?"

Bolívar collaborated with the Argentine revolutionary José de San Martín to liberate Perú. The 'Upper Peru' – the northern section of Perú – was also liberated and received the name of Bolivia, in honor of Bolívar. At different times, Bolívar served as a president or 'dictator' of Venezuela, Colombia, and Peru, but post-war life with its political battles and rivalry scared him. "I am more afraid of peace than of war!" he complained. Indeed, the independence fighter warlords who won battles for Bolívar considered the lands they liberated as their 'own,' so after the battle of Carabobo, Bolívar had to divide Venezuela into 3 military districts to let his generals 'rule' their regions. Still the civil war conflicts kept erupting. To stop infighting, Bolívar's friends proposed to make him an "emperor of the Andes," with an empire covering most former Spanish colonies. But Bolívar refused. "I am not Napoleon," he said, "nor do I wish to be. Neither do I want to imitate Caesar..." In a letter to his friend, General Sucre he wrote: "I am ready to meet the Spaniards in a battle to end war in America, but nothing more. I feel tired, I am old, and I have nothing to expect."

In 1822 Bolívar met his future girlfriend, Manuela Sáenz. Manuela was a revolutionary and independence fighter who participated in the conspiracy against the viceroy of Perú by recruiting Royalist soldiers to join the rebel army of José de San Martín. Manuela was popular among independence fighters. She usually wore a colonel's uniform and addressed rebel troops with patriotic speeches. In 1828, following a conflict with Bolívar over presidential powers and the constitution of Colombia, a group of liberal conspirators invaded the presidential palace in Bogotá planning to assassinate Bolívar with daggers – the way Caesar was assassinated. Bolívar heard them coming and was prepared to face them, but Manuela convinced him to jump out of the window instead, and told the conspirators Bolívar was somewhere in the building. Then she led them from room to room to room, until they realized they had been tricked. They beat up Manuela and left.

Endless political clashes with different cliques of independence fighters exhausted Bolívar. He was sick with tuberculosis and his health was failing. Meanwhile Perú invaded Ecuador, Venezuela seceded from Gran Colombia, Bolívar's generals kept staging revolts... Bolívar's dream of the 'United States of South America" was fading. He resigned from his presidential post in Colombia and had to sell his remaining property to support himself. The fight between Bolívar's supporters and opponents was looking more and more like a civil war, and Bolívar decided to go into exile and settle in Europe. In December of 1830 he received the news that one of his most loyal friends, General Sucre, whom he had trained to be his successor, had been murdered. It was the last blow to Bolívar. He died a few days later, at the age of 47.

Manuela Sáenz

The official cause of Bolívar's death was tuberculosis, but there were rumors that he had been poisoned. Reviewing the records of Bolívar's doctors, some modern scientists suggested that he may have been killed by arsenic. Arsenic is a powerful poison, but it also could be found in large concentrations in natural water in the Andes mountains, as well as in 19th-century medicines. In 2010 Venezuelan President Hugo Chávez ordered the exhumation (removal from the grave) of Bolívar's remains to find out. But the experts who studied them could neither support nor reject the poisoning hypothesis.

Bolívar's house in Bogotá, Colombia

Laskarina Bouboulina
1771 – 1825

Greece was a province of the Ottoman Turkish Empire from the fall of Constantinople in 1453 until the success of the Greek Revolution of 1821. The Greek independence movement grew in the 18th century, encouraged by the success of the wars Russia waged against Turkey. Russian Tsar Peter the Great called on Orthodox Christians throughout Europe to rise against the Ottomans for "faith and homeland." During the reign of the Russian Empress Catherine the Great, Greek ships joined the Russian fleet in campaigns against the Ottoman Navy. In 1770 Russian Admiral Alexey Orlov brought the Russian fleet to the Mani Peninsula in Southern Greece to support an independence uprising – now known as the Orlov Revolt. Even though Russians defeated the Turkish navy, the Orlov Revolt was suppressed and many Greek rebels were captured. Among them were Stavrianos Pinotsis, a captain from the island of Hydra, and his wife Skevo. In a prison in Constantinople, Skevo gave birth to a baby girl who was destined to become a naval commander and a heroine of the Greek War of Independence – Laskarina Bouboulina.

Laskarina's dad died in prison, and her mom returned to Greece, remarried, and moved to the island of Spetses. Laskarina's step-dad, Dimitris Lazarou, was also an independence fighter. He changed his name to Lazarou-Orlov to commemorate his participation in the Orlov Revolt and pledged loyalty to Russia. He was also a fan of the Russian Empress Catherine the Great and believed that women can make great leaders. So, rather than learning how to cook and sew, Laskarina was taught sailing, navigation, and even basic military skills. She also loved the songs of Greek klephts – the anti-Ottoman rebels and bandits who lived in the mountains.

"Russian fleet destroys Ottoman ships in the Battle of Chios (the Orlov Revolt)" by Ivan Aivazovsky

At 17 Laskarina married a ship captain. They had 3 kids, but then her husband perished fighting against Algerian pirates. At 30 Laskarina married again. Her new husband was a wealthy shipowner, Captain Dimitrios Bouboulis, a Greek independence fighter who participated in the Russian-Turkish war on the side of Russia. Laskarina took his name, becoming Laskarina Bouboulina. In 1811 he, too, died in a battle with Algerian pirates, leaving Bouboulina a vast fortune and his trading business. In 1816 the Ottoman authorities tried to confiscate (seize) Bouboulina's property because her husband had fought on the side of Russia. Bouboulina managed to save her fortune from confiscation by appealing to the sultan's mother. But while the government was considering her case, she contacted the Russian ambassador in Constantinople, and he arranged for her to stay for a few months in Crimea.

In 1774, the Ottoman Empire was defeated by the Russian troops of Catherine the Great. The Crimean peninsula and many other territories on the North coast of the Black Sea became part of the Russian Empire. These areas – Novorossia, the 'New Russia' – had large Greek communities that had lived there since the times of Ancient Greece and the Byzantine Empire. Russians encouraged the revival of Greek culture. The new coastal province received the official name of Taurida (after the ancient Greek name of Crimea – Tauris). In Taurida, Catherine the Great founded new cities, giving them the names of ancient Greek colonies or new names in Greek – Odessa, Sevastopol, Simferopol...The Odessa port became a center of Greek culture and business, and that's where, in 1814, Greek patriots founded the famous secret society Filiki Eteria ("Society of Friends") whose goal was the revival of the Byzantine Empire with Constantinople as the capital. Historians believe that, while staying in Crimea, Bouboulina met with the leadership of Filiki Eteria and decided to honor her husband's memory by continuing his fight for Greek independence. At that point Bouboulina was 45, and immensely rich. She had 7 kids plus 3 step children, and most of them were already grownups. The Filiki Eteria expanded explosively, recruiting members in Greece and abroad. The Greek War of Independence was approaching.

Bouboulina's ship, 'Agamemnon'

Two years later, Bouboulina ordered the construction of a ship that was larger than most ships in the Ottoman fleet and therefore not allowed by the Ottoman regulations. The news of this reached Constantinople, and an admiral of the Ottoman Navy was sent to check what she was up to. But Bouboulina promptly bribed the admiral and was left alone. The spectacular 18-cannon warship was built and named 'Agamemnon.' Bouboulina also purchased weapons for the patriots of the Greek islands of Hydra, Insara, and Spetses, hid them in her house on Spetses, and transported them to the rebels on her merchant ships. Ships from the islands of Spezios, Hydra and Psara formed the core of the Greek naval force. On March 13, 1821, twelve days before the official start of the war, Bouboulina raised a Greek flag on the Agamemnon. It was the flag of the Comnenus dynasty of Byzantine emperors. The captain of Agamemnon was Bouboulina's son Yiannis. With 8 ships, Bouboulina began a naval blockade of the Ottoman fortress in the coastal Greek city of Nafplion.

"Next to her, the indecisive became strong, and the courageous retreated before her," the Greek historian Philemon wrote about Bouboulina. An eyewitness of the Nafplio blockade, historian Anargyros Hatzi-Anargyrou, recalled "… indeed the very rare event in the history of nations of a woman to take up arms, a very rich woman who decided to offer her ships, her money, and her sons as a sacrifice to the altar of her country. This woman is Laskarina Bouboulina, whom people around the world salute as a heroine. She had the heart of a lion. As I recall, on her own vessel, she alone gave the orders for the boats to attack the fort. They immediately attack but a rain of bullets and cannon fire from the coastal fortifications make her brave lads fall back for a moment. Like an angry Amazon watching the battle from the deck of her boat she then shouts… 'What are you – ladies? Not men? Forward!'"

During the siege of Nafplion, Bouboulina's son Yiannis left to bring troops from Argos and was killed in a battle. It is said that Bouboulina searched the battlefield for his body and sent a message back to Spetses, "My son is dead, but Argos is ours." During Yiannis' funeral Bouboulina personally executed 3 Turkish prisoners. Meanwhile, the uprising spread throughout Greece. Bouboulina equipped over 80 ships – all on her own money, uniting the forces from many islands into powerful fleets. The Greek fight for independence gave rise to a movement of sympathy and solidarity across Europe and in the Americas known as **Philhellenism** ("the love of Greek culture"). Volunteers from European countries and Russia arrived in Greece joining the rebels. The most famous among them was the English poet Lord Byron who fought and perished in Greece.

"Greek War of Independence" by Georg Perlberg

Bouboulina became a star. Every newspaper published reports about her battles and pictures that portrayed her as a stunning Greek goddess. Once a French volunteer showed Bouboulina a print he had bought in Paris that depicted her in the middle of a naval battle. Her 'portrait' was so far from reality that Boubolina couldn't stop laughing. In Bouboulina's house on the island of Spetses, which is now a museum, there is a Russian folk print showing Bouboulina on horseback with the caption, "The famous widow Bobelina surpasses many women in her courage and strength. She is 30, and you can tell that in her youth she was very beautiful. She rides her horse in a dress appropriate to her. Under her new Greek banners she defends the island of Thasos where Turks used to get wood for building their ships."

In September 1821, during the siege of the Greek town of Tripolitsa (present-day Tripoli) by the troops of Greek general Theodoros Kolokotronis, the sultan's mother asked Bouboulina to help negotiate the release of the wives and harem women of the local Turkish officials from the besieged city. Bouboulina made it happen. Tripolitsa was captured, and the Greek fleets won a number of naval battles against the Ottoman navy in the Aegean Sea. The war was ruthless. When either side captured a town, all its population was massacred and all the property looted. In 1822 Ottoman troops slaughtered and enslaved over 100 thousand Greek residents of the island of Chios. In revenge, Greek Independence fighter Constantine Kanaris destroyed he flagship of the Turkish Navy by ramming a 'fire ship' (a boat loaded with fuel and set on fire) into it. Powder kegs on the Turkish ship blew up sending it into the air in a gigantic explosion that killed 2000 sailors and naval officers on board.

"The burning of the Turkish flagship by Kanaris" by Nikiforos Lytras

Bouboulina's critics accused her of letting her troops loot the Muslim quarters of Tripolitsa, and when Nafplion fell they accused her of taking a lot of Ottoman property for herself. Disagreements among different groups of independence fighters soon turned into civil wars. The residents of mainland Greece and shipowners from the islands clashed with the people from the Peloponnese peninsula. These civil wars lasted from 1823 to 1825, weakening the Greek forces. Bouboulina participated in these wars, but after her faction lost, her house in Nafplion was confiscated, and she returned to the island of Spetses.

It was reported that at home on Spetses Bouboulina cooked all her food herself, afraid of being poisoned. Her concerns were well-grounded. At some point her political opponents accused her of witchcraft, and she spent some time in jail. In May 1825 Bouboulina's son Georgios Yiannouzas shared with her a plan to elope (run away in order to get married against the wishes of one's family) with a girl he loved. The girl was Eugenia Koutsi from Spetses. Her parents knew that she wanted to marry Georgios, but they were Bouboulina's political enemies, so they ordered their daughter to get engaged to another man. Bouboulina gave Georgios and Eugenia her blessing and they eloped. Looking for Eugenia, the enraged and armed members of the Koutsi family came to Bouboulina's house. When she walked out onto a balcony to talk to them, she was shot and killed. Bouboulina was 54 when she died. A few days after her death, a Russian delegation arrived in Spetses to present Bouboulina with the honorary rank of Admiral of the Russian fleet. Her ship, Agamemnon, was renamed 'Spetses' and continued serving as the flagship of the Greek Navy.

"The last battle of the defenders of Missolonghi" by Theodoros Vryzakis

At the time of Bouboulina's death the tide of the independence war was about to turn in favor of the Ottoman Empire. The Sultan asked Muhammad Ali, the Ottoman governor of Egypt, for help, promising him the island of Crete if his troops could suppress the Greek revolt. Muhammad Ali's son, Ibrahim Pasha, arrived in Greece with a modern, well-trained and equipped Egyptian army. Before long he brought the Peloponnese peninsula under Egyptian control. After a year-long siege, the town of Missolonghi fell, and the Turks captured Athens. The cause of Greek independence was almost lost, when Russia, Britain, and France sent their warships to help Greek rebels in 1827. The Ottoman–Egyptian fleet was sunk in the naval battle of Navarino, the Ottoman troops in the Peloponnese surrendered, and independence fighters retook central Greece. In 1829 the Ottoman Empire declared war on Russia and the Russian army marched on Constantinople. The Ottoman government was forced to sign the Treaty of Adrianople in which it promised autonomy for Greece, Serbia, and Romania. In 1832 the borders of Greece were established and Prince Otto of Bavaria became the first king of Greece.

"The naval Battle of Navarino" by Ivan Aivazovsky and "Bouboulina at Napflion," unkown artist, 19th century

JOSÉ MARTÍ
1853 – 1895

José Martí was born to Spanish parents. His dad was an artillery officer who served in Cuba, a colony ruled by a Spanish viceroy. Cuba's sugar cane and coffee plantations were among the richest in the world. Huge numbers of African slaves were sold to Cuba every year. But in the mid-19th century new farming techniques emerged and made slave labor unnecessary. In many areas in the Americas and West Indies, keeping slaves became more expensive than paying salaries to seasonal workers. Plantation owners who failed to modernize their business went broke. Others started bringing Chinese workers to Cuba, expecting slavery to be abolished any moment. As a result, Afro-Cubans were becoming desperately poor, and business owners demanded reforms from the Spanish government. A revolutionary mood was on the rise.

"I grow a white rose" by José Martí

I grow a white rose
Both in June and in January,
For a sincere friend
Who shakes my hand with an open mind.
And for a cruel one,
Who wants to tear the heart
From my chest,
I grow neither thistles nor thorns –
I grow a white rose.

When José Martí was 12, he was enrolled in a Havana school whose principal, Rafael de Mendive, was a patriot and supporter of Cuban independence. Mendive encouraged Martí's interest in writing and politics. In 1868, when José Martí was 15, the Ten Years' War broke out – the anti-colonial uprising that united the Creoles (people of Spanish descent born in Cuba), Afro-Cubans (descendants of African slaves) and Mulattos (mixed-race people). The rebels, nicknamed *mambí*, attacked Spanish colonial troops from the mountainous areas of Cuba. The Spanish sent agents with checkbooks from New York and Madrid banks hoping to bribe mambí leaders, but they refused bribes. Patriotic Creoles freed the slaves who joined rebel troops, and the numbers of mambí grew.

"Cuban mambi" vintage photo

To attract liberal Cubans to their side, Spaniards granted the island freedom of the press, speech, and assembly. However, when newspapers called for independence, they were instantly closed by the authorities. So, out of nowhere, there appeared dozens of brand-new publications calling for independence. They were all closed, of course, but not before their first issue was published and distributed! José Martí started publishing his own newspaper – *La Patria Libre*. Meanwhile, Cubans loyal to Spain organized armed units of **Volunteers** to defend their plantations and towns from the mambí. With sabers drawn and guns loaded, they marched around Havana, beating up or shooting anyone who was suspected of sympathizing with the rebels. One day they broke into Principal Mendive's apartment and found there 'evidence' of treason. Mendive was arrested and thrown in jail. His school was closed. José tried to enroll in another school, but the Volunteers threatened its principal, and José's application was rejected.

One day José and his best friend Fermín Dominguez, the son of a wealthy lawyer, ran into their former classmate from Rafael Mendive's school. The guy was wearing the uniform of a lieutenant of the Spanish army. Upset that their classmate had betrayed the independence cause so cherished by Mendive's students, José and Fermín wrote a letter to him, reading: "Comrade, have you ever dreamed of the glory of a traitor? Do you know how traitors have been punished since times immemorial? We believe that you, as a former student of Señor Mendive, will give an explanation in response to this letter."

Havana – 19th-century photo;
José Martí on gold Cuban peso, 1916

Soon after, José and Fermín were at Fermín's house exchanging jokes with girls who lived across the street. In Old Havana the streets are narrow, and neighbors often chat with one another across the street. Suddenly there was the sound of drums. A Volunteer battalion appeared around the corner. Fermín dropped an orange peel out the window, and it landed on the hat of one of the Volunteers. The Volunteers broke into Fermín's house and arrested José and Fermín. They also found copies of *La Patria Libre*, maps of Cuba with symbols of the fighting in the east, and a draft letter to the kid who joined the Spanish Army.

In court the prosecutor asked José and Fermín, "Who wrote this letter?" The friends rose together. "But you couldn't write one letter at the same time!" To save his friend, José stepped forward. "I wrote it alone." So, the verdict read, "For insulting the honor of the First Battalion of Volunteers, Jose Martí, 17 years old, is sentenced to 6 years of hard labor; Fermín Dominguez, 18 years old, is sentenced to 6 months imprisonment..."

In jail José, wearing a prisoner's uniform and wooden shoes, was chained to a ring in the wall of an underground dungeon. Hard labor wrecked people, but it wasn't the worst. Many prisoners were tortured – by water, fire, light, darkness... In sound torture, prisoners were locked in a stone cave. In the huge hall in front of the cave, other prisoners sounded the alarm. The acoustics of the cave multiplied the sound, and people lost their mind after a few hours. Those who died in jail were not buried – their bodies were discarded through special chutes into the sea, where schools of Caribbean sharks kept an ominous watch.

Old Havana today

José was sent to work in the San Lazaro quarries – giant holes in the limestone core of the island. There were puddles of sewage at the bottom of the quarries, and a dust that never settled ate into the eyes. After a few weeks in the quarries, José began to go blind. He turned into a shadow with rattling chains. Finally, in Havana, José's dad, through some army connections, got introduced to the owner of the San Lazaro quarries! The guy turned out to be a good-natured man and promised to help. José was transferred to the Isle of Pines to work on construction projects along with African slaves under "strict supervision." But once on the island, José was asked to tutor kids and do occasional errands. All went well until the rumors of his good luck reached Havana, and in 1871 the authorities ordered to deport him from Cuba to Spain.

Surprisingly, in Spain the 'criminal' José Martí was just let go! Soon he connected with other political exiles from Cuba, including his friend Fermín Dominguez. Martí published some materials about the horrors of San Lazaro and the fight for Cuban independence, but, to his shock, even the Spanish liberals didn't care about the tragedy in Cuba. They were preoccupied with domestic affairs. Indeed, clouds were gathering over the Spanish monarchy. Following the mutinies of sailors and artillerymen in Cadiz, on February 9, 1873, the king abdicated (left the throne) and the Second Spanish Republic was proclaimed. However, contrary to José Martí's expectations, the new republican government wasn't planning to let Cuba have its independence. So, Martí got in touch with the Cuban Revolutionary Committee in New York, offering them help. For years Cuban revolutionaries hoped that the "great democracy of the north," the United States, would help them gain independence. But they ended up deceived. The US proposed to purchase Cuba, and when the Spanish rejected their offer, the US sided with Spain against the Cuban rebels. American troops blockaded the island, detaining ships that carried rifles for the mambí.

In 1875 José Martí traveled to Mexico to see his family who had moved there. José met local liberal politicians and journalists supporting the Cuban rebels, and started writing for local newspapers. He made his living teaching French, English, Italian, and German languages and literature, and was able to rent a better home for his family. In 1877, José sailed to Cuba with a fake passport and discovered that the rebels had lost the Ten Years' War. 200,000 people had perished in that war. Hundreds of villages and plantations had been burned to the ground. Most of the patriots were in exile, locked up in prisons or sentenced to hard labor.

To bring an end to the war, the Spanish promised to declare a general amnesty (forgiveness of criminal actions) and free slaves who fought in the rebel groups. They also came up with five million pesos in gold to bribe rebels who agreed to surrender. The rebels knew from where that gold came. It had been accumulated by the Spaniards through the plunder of Cuba. Yet the war was lost, and they laid down their arms. One of the reasons for their defeat was the weakening of support among Creole plantation owners. Fighting side-by-side with white revolutionaries empowered the African slaves. So the plantation elites were afraid that the war could become a "black war," in which the slaves would turn against their former owners and make Cuba into a 'second Haiti,' a 'black republic.'

Antonio Maceo; José Martí's wife Carmen and their son in 1895; Cuban mambí

Back in Mexico, José Martí married the girl he was in love with – Carmen, a daughter of a wealthy Cuban plantation owner. Once the amnesty was announced, they moved to Havana where José hoped to get in touch with the mambí heroes of the Ten Years' War, Afro-Cuban rebel leader Juan Gualberto Gómez, and the 'bronze titan,' another Afro-Cuban, General Antonio Maceo. Once the mambí leaders started trusting Martí, he was admitted to secret meetings of the Cuban revolutionaries and learned that they were preparing a new uprising. The new independence movement was led by Cuban exiles in New York who arranged the purchase of weapons for the rebels.

Elegant young Cubans sailed from Cuba to the US on mail ships. Their crocodile-skin suitcases contained thousands of pesos collected by island patriots to buy rifles. Then, under the cover of night, boats loaded with weapons and ammunition arrived at the shores of Oriente province, Cuba. The captains steered them in total darkness following a signal that came from the shore – the blowing of a conch shell. In the port of Havana where they unloaded ships bringing textiles from New York, whenever workers noticed a package stained with red paint, they sent for a muscular African who carried it in an unknown direction. These packages were hard to lift – they contained rifles and cartridges.

Carmen and José had a son, but Carmen was stressed and rarely happy. Her dad suspected that José was again entangled with the revolutionaries, and demanded that his daughter return home. Rebellious slaves had burned his plantations, and he was angry that José's independence ideas included equality for Creoles and Africans.

One day, at Havana train station, workers dropped a box bound for Santiago de Cuba in the East. It was marked with red paint, and, as it broke, rifle cartridges scattered across the station platform. As a result, hundreds of patriots in Santiago de Cuba were arrested. Maceo and other rebel military leaders decided to start an uprising ahead of schedule and attacked Spanish military barracks in Santiago de Cuba. The war began, but instead of a simultaneous uprising on the entire island, only one province rose up. The revolt was doomed.

José Martí was arrested too, but Cuban authorities were afraid to throw him in jail, because he was already well-known in Europe, the United States, and Latin America as a poet, and an author of a few books. So Martí was deported to Spain – again under the usual 'strict supervision.' Since the Spanish authorities preferred to 'supervise' rum and cigars smuggled from Cuba into Spain, and couldn't care less about Cuban exiles, Martí was soon free, and in 1880, he came to New York. From this moment on he dedicated all his time to the cause of Cuban liberation, publishing magazines, books, poetry, and working with the New York Cuban revolutionaries' committee. There were many wealthy Cubans in New York. Wearing his only suit, Martí visited them asking for donations to buy more weapons for the Cuban rebels. Most often he walked – he couldn't afford a horse-drawn streetcar ticket. It cost five cents, as did a cup of coffee. José Martí invited Carmen with their baby to New York, and Carmen came, but a life of poverty and around-the-clock revolutionary activity upset her. She and the baby left for Havana and José Martí never saw them again.

For years Martí traveled through the United States, Central America, and the Caribbean, working to unify pro-independence Cuban political clubs, groups, and secret societies into the Cuban Revolutionary Party. Eventually, this party brought together all Cuban social and racial groups in the struggle for independence and freedom. Finally, an invasion of Cuba and a new uprising were scheduled – for February 24, 1895, the first day of the traditional carnival, when the Spanish authorities were most likely to be distracted. Indeed, on the appointed day, a band of 24 armed rebels appeared in the province of Matanzas, and even more were seen in Santa Clara. There were 20,000 Spanish troops in Cuba, plus 60,000 Volunteers. The initial uprising outbreaks were suppressed, but in the mountainous Santiago de Cuba a guerilla war continued. In April General Maceo arrived from Costa Rica, then Martí and Gomez came from Santo Domingo on Hispaniola. Now that the leaders of the uprising were all in Cuba, their army grew rapidly, reaching 6000 men.

However, the true mastermind of this independence revolution, José Martí, didn't live to see its victory. It was decided that Martí should return to the United States to buy more weapons for his fighters. After Gomez and Martí parted in the Oriente province, Martí was ambushed by the Spanish forces and killed in the Battle of Dos Ríos – the Battle of Two Rivers. The Spanish quickly identified Martí's body and buried him in a nearby village. But a day later there came an order from Havana to exhume Martí's body and deliver it to Santiago de Cuba, to be buried 'with honors' in the best local cemetery. Martí was too famous to be quietly discarded.

José Martí and his son; José Martí monument in Havana

The success of the Cuban War of Independence was sealed 7 years later, when the United States entered the war in 1898. By this time many areas of Cuba were in the hands of the independence fighters, even though Spain sent over 200,000 soldiers to suppress the uprising. In Havana, however, it was quiet until 1898, when riots broke out and the US sent a battleship, the USS Maine, to protect Americans living in the city. In Havana Harbor the ship was destroyed by a powerful explosion that killed its crew. The cause of the explosion was never identified, but American media – newspapers and magazines, that strongly influenced public opinion – blamed it on the Spanish and demanded to settle scores with Spain. Suddenly all newspapers were full of reports about 'atrocities' performed by the colonial Spanish government in Cuba. Famous newspaper publisher William Hearst asked his Cuban war correspondent Frederic Remington, who was a well-known artist and illustrator, to send him pictures of 'atrocities' from Cuba. Remington replied in a telegram, "Everything is quiet here in Havana. There is no trouble. No war." But Remington responded, "You provide the pictures, and I'll provide the war." So American troops were sent to Cuba to support Cuban independence fighters and 'end the civil war.' Spain had already lost the Philippines and Puerto Rico to the United States. Unwilling to fight yet another war, the Spanish signed a peace treaty that granted Cuba independence.

American cartoon published in 1898

MICHAEL COLLINS
1890 – 1922

The hero of the Irish War of Independence, Michael Collins, was viewed as a 'living legend' already during his lifetime. He had a nickname – the Big Fella – but he wasn't particularly tall. The nickname reflected his 'big' personality. Collins was a celebrity both in Ireland and in Britain, against whose 700-year-long domination of Ireland he fought. After he died – young, at 31 – he joined the ranks of historical figures seen as 'saints,' or 'martyrs,' of independence movements around the globe. Michael Collins, José Martí, Che Guevara – all were charismatic leaders with a certain mystery about them. They all were controversial figures – seen as either freedom fighters or terrorists. They all died young, and they all still fascinate thousands of people worldwide.

Michael Collins was born in West Cork, Ireland. His dad, a carpenter and tenant farmer, sympathized with the ***Irish Republican Brotherhood*** (IRB) – a secret organization of Irish independence fighters seeking to force the British Empire out of Ireland. He even agreed with some IRB activists who suggested that organizing terrorist acts in England was a valid method of guerilla war against the British. The Irish countryside was devastated by poverty and mass emigration to the United States. Part of the problem was that English laws protected land owners at the expense of their 'tenants' – people who actually worked on the farms. Many landowners lived in England and Scotland, since most of the land in Ireland was confiscated from Irish Catholics and given to English and Scottish Protestants in the 16th and 17th centuries. The memories of the Great Irish Famine (1845-1852) that killed over 1 million people were still fresh. Michael Collins' dad remembered how, during the famine, English landlords were exporting food from Ireland to England.

Death Positivity Bias

'Death positivity bias' is a sociological term used to explain why people often have more favorable opinions of dead leaders than of living ones, and why so many historical figures seen as heroes are people who died young. Death seems to elevate the status of historical figures in the eyes of the public, especially if it's an untimely death in a battle, through assassination, or execution.

Even though Michael Collins grew up hating the British Empire, rural Ireland offered very few opportunities, so at 16 Collins went to London and worked there as a clerk at a bank. In London he was shocked at how little both British elites and common citizens cared about the dreadful situation in Ireland. During the First World War Collins returned to Ireland. He saw the war as an opportunity – it would drain the resources of the empire, making it easier to free Ireland of British rule. The event that opened the Irish War of Independence was the so-called 'Easter Rising' in Dublin, in 1916 – a rebellion organized by the Irish Republican Brotherhood and other pro-independence groups. The uprising was ruthlessly suppressed. Hundreds of people perished in clashes with the British forces, Dublin was in ruins, dozens were imprisoned and executed. Thrown in jail for participation in the Easter Rising, Michael Collins emerged as a leader of the rebel prisoners. He shared his knowledge of military tactics, organized *Gaelic*-language classes, and negotiated with prison authorities.

Tenant Farmer

Tenant farmers don't own the land. They farm on the land they rent. 'Tenant' comes from the Latin verb **tenēre** = to hold, to keep.

In 1917, when the Easter Rising activists were released from prisons under an amnesty, they took control of **Sinn Féin** – a pro-independence Irish party founded in 1905 by Irish politician Arthur Griffith. Michael Collins won a seat in the British Parliament as an MP (member of Parliament) for Sinn Féin.

Gaelic

Gaelic, or Irish Gaelic, is the Irish language. It belongs to the Celtic language family. In the 19th century English became dominant in Ireland. To preserve Gaelic, Irish patriots started the Gaelic Revival movement encouraging the everyday use of Gaelic language and the study of Gaelic literature.

The Irish rebels and the British troops, during the Easter Rising in Dublin

IRA member on a rooftop

Collins was also busy building an intelligence network for the independence rebels, recruiting dozens of Irish who worked for the British government in Dublin and in London. These 'agents' warned Collins of the raids and arrests planned by the British police. With the help of his spy network Collins organized a prison break for Éamon de Valera – the future president of independent Ireland. His agents smuggled key cutting tools and blanks for keys to prison inmates in fruit cakes. Collins also trained assassins to target British intelligence and police agents.

On January 21, 1919, Sinn Féin MPs, including Michael Collins, refused to take their seats in the House of Commons of the British Parliament in London and formed their own parliament – **Dáil Éireann** – and a **shadow government**. This was equivalent to declaring independence.

Michael Collins, Éamon de Valera

Sinn Féin = *'We, ourselves,'* in Gaelic

Éamon de Valera arrested

A revolutionary paramilitary organization – he *Irish Republican Army (IRA)* – was formed. Tens of thousands joined and trained for guerilla warfare. Michael Collins first served as the Minister of Finance in the Irish shadow government, but soon he became the Intelligence Director of the IRA and focused on organizing *sabotage*, assassinations, hit-and-run ambushes, and raids on British soldiers in Ireland. His elite strike force was called 'the Squad,' a group of snipers, all members of the Irish Republican Brotherhood.

To crush Collins' spy and assassin network, the British government sent to Ireland military intelligence and sabotage teams of their own – the *Black and Tans* and the *Cairo Gang*. Arriving in Dublin in September 1920, the Cairo Gang tried to track down Michael Collins and infiltrate (penetrate) his agent network. All their attempts failed. They couldn't even trace his movement around Dublin. As if mocking them, Collins casually stopped for drinks with friends at various city hotels and pubs, and by the time the British agents learned about this, he was gone.

Shadow Government

A 'shadow government' is a group of political opposition leaders who organize themselves into a structure that mimics the actual government of their country. A shadow government prepares to rule the country once the opposition gains power.

to sabotage = to deliberately destroy or damage property, to obstruct or stop work in order to achieve political or military goals

Some of the Squad members; Below: The Cairo Gang

Batt O'Connor, one of Collins' comrades-in-arms, wrote in his 1929 memoir, "On one occasion when the Sinn Féin headquarters was raided, Michael Collins was in an office he had in that building. He succeeded in bluffing the first policeman who came into the office. Pretending he was an unimportant assistant clerk, he walked out of the office, skipped lightly up the stairs to the floor above and escaped through a skylight." Yet another time when British agents tracked him down, Collins escaped by climbing out of his office onto the roof. He ran from roof to roof, jumped into a skylight over a stairwell at a hotel on the same block, then walked out of the hotel calmly, looking like one of the guests, and joined the crowd in the street watching the raid on his office.

The British were desperate to lay their hands on Collins' intelligence files, but every time they searched his offices, they found nothing. Batt O'Connor came up with endless variations on secret spaces that housed Collins' papers. "The house was turned upside down," he recalled one raid. "All the floors were pulled up and the trimmings of doors and windows stripped. The search lasted 22 hours, but although the woodwork under my cupboard [where Collins' documents were hidden] was broken in, nothing was found. I built it a foot or two above the floor, with a false back, behind which was the hiding place." Collins rarely praised his men. He was known to say, "Why should I thank people for doing their part? Isn't Ireland their country as well as mine?" Yet for saving his documents, he thanked O'Connor, and added, "If they had got them, they would have beaten us in a few weeks. All our plans and our best men would have become known to them."

Here is another account of Collins' narrow escape, also from Batt O'Connor's memoir: "Returning from the countryside where he was attending to military matters, he found a cordon of military, who were stopping and searching all incoming cars. Without waiting to be questioned, he stepped out of his car, walked to the officer in charge and began chatting with him. They became quite friendly as Michael sympathized with him on the unpleasantness of his job. From a silver cigarette case he offered the officer a cigarette. While this little comedy was being played, the soldiers were searching Collins' car and questioning other men who were in it. Coming back to the officer they saluted: "Car and passengers all right, Sir." They didn't think of searching the man who was talking and laughing with their officer. The papers and maps were in his pockets."

Unable to catch Collins, the Cairo Gang focused on hunting down Irish republican leaders, and after a couple failed assassination attempts they finally succeeded. A republican activist from Limerick, John Lynch, was murdered when he was asleep in his bed. A few independent activists were seized by the Gang and killed at Dublin Castle. In response, Michael Collins ordered the execution of the entire Cairo Gang. He had post office workers steal the mail arriving from London. The mail was read and analyzed. Soon Collins had a list of the Dublin addresses of the Cairo Gang members. Early on Sunday morning, November 21, eight assassination teams of the Squad broke into the homes of 19 British officers. A few were dragged out of their houses and put against the wall for a firing squad execution, but most were killed in bed, in their pajamas, some – in front of their wives. To show Collins what his actions would cost Ireland, that afternoon, British soldiers showed up at a football game between Dublin and Tipperary at Dublin's Croke Park stadium, and machine-gunned 13 spectators and the Tipperary goalkeeper. They also killed 2 political prisoners and a random guy arrested for curfew violation, who happened to be in jail.

A massive reward was promised for the assassination of Collins. He was now the 'most wanted man in the British empire.' The British authorities told their agents that, if caught, Collins should not be arrested, but shot. He slept with a revolver under his pillow. Despite this, Michael Collins came to the funeral of the Croke Park victims and helped carry the coffins. By 1921 the Irish guerilla war against the British was in full swing, and both sides relied heavily on terrorism and executions. A certain Mrs. Lindsay gave away to the British the hiding place of 12 IRA members who were ambushed and killed. In revenge the IRA executed her husband. Irish journalist Tim Pat Coogan tells the story of how Michael Collins

Michael Collins; Black & Tans raiding party leaving Dungarvan Castle in 1920

ordered his father to execute two girls who dated British soldiers and passed to them information about the IRA. His dad disobeyed the order. When accused of engaging in terrorism, Michael Collins pointed out that all liberation movements throughout history had done this, and that he only used this method against select targets, 'sentenced to death' for their crimes, never against random civilians.

As the war dragged on, Collins became more and more pessimistic. He stopped believing his Republicans could win. There was a shortage of arms and ammunition. "We had an average of one round of ammunition for each weapon," Collins recalled later. Many IRA fighters were exhausted and losing hope. Plus, Collins felt that "the net was closing" around him. The British tracked down and arrested a few of his agents.

The same year Michael Collins proposed to Catherine ('Kitty') Kiernan, whose family supported independence fighters. Soon they got engaged, but their marriage was not destined to happen. Collins had only one year left to live.

Meanwhile, in London, the British government was under pressure to 'do something' about the war in Ireland. British troops were dying, and the public was outraged. So, the British Prime Minister, David Lloyd George, reached out to the Irish shadow government offering truce and inviting them to London to negotiate on a peace treaty.

Kitty Kiernan in March 1922; Winston Churchill

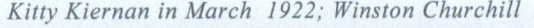

Michael Collins didn't want to go to London. He knew that the Irish wouldn't get everything they wanted and was afraid that he would end up being blamed for the results. But Éamon de Valera, the President of the Dáil Éireann and the only man in Ireland more powerful than Collins, ordered him to go. In the fall of 1921 Michael Collins arrived in London and, to his utter shock, discovered that over there he was a huge celebrity. Nobody seemed to remember that only recently he had been the 'bloodthirsty monster murdering British soldiers.' Instead, newspapers described him as handsome, charming, and mysterious. High-society ladies tried to meet him and invited him to parties. Collins exchanged letters with his fiancee, Kitty, every other day, but she complained that his letters were composed 'in great haste,' and that 'the first and best goes to Ireland, I am only a good second.'

The head of the Irish delegation was Arthur Griffith, but he was often sick, and Collins carried out most of the negotiations, working closely with the British Colonial Secretary Winston Churchill. One day, in Churchill's office, recalling the spy wars in Dublin, Collins said: "You hunted me night and day. You put a price on my head." "Wait a minute, you are not the only one with the price on your head," replied Churchill. He took from his office wall the framed copy of the reward offered for his capture by the Boers during the Second Boer War in South Africa. "I offered for your head a good price – £5,000," he said. "Now look at what they offered for my head – £25 dead or alive. How would you like that?" In his memoir Churchill wrote that, hearing that, Collins burst out laughing. "We had a really serviceable conversation," recalled Churchill, "and thereafter – though I must admit that deep in my heart there was a certain gulf between us – we never to the best of my belief lost the basis of a common understanding."

Churchill was just one of the 'soldiers' in the charm offensive on Collins. Other London celebrities flattered him and sought his friendship as well. Well-known London upper class circles portrait-painter Sir John Lavery was all over Collins. Lavery painted the portraits of both Collins and Arthur Griffith. Lavery's American-born wife, Hazel, told all her girlfriends that Collins had a crush on her. London literary celebrity, J. M. Barrie, author of "Peter Pan," sought Collins' friendship, as well as the Llewelyn Davies family whose kids inspired Barrie to write "Peter Pan."

A Charm Offensive = *a campaign of flattery and friendliness whose goal is to make the target of the 'offensive' agree to something*

The treaty negotiated in London ended up both a blessing and a disaster for Ireland, just as Michael Collins predicted. The 26 Southern, Catholic, counties of Ireland were to become the *Irish Free State*. It would be ruled by a government in Dublin, but remain part of the British Empire. The six Northern (predominantly Protestant) counties were to stay in the United Kingdom. The British government threatened to resume war if this offer was rejected. The night Collins signed the treaty, he wrote in his diary: "Today I signed my death warrant." He suspected that he and Griffith had been 'set up' by de Valera to carry the blame for any shortcomings in the peace treaty. On the other hand, he was convinced that the British offer was, indeed, final. He referred to it as "Not freedom but the power to achieve freedom." According to Churchill, the last time they saw each other in London, Collins said, "I shall not last long. My life is forfeit, but I shall do my best. After I am gone it will be easier for others." Collins was grateful to Churchill, who, he believed, made the Treaty happen. "Tell Winston we could never have done anything without him," he wrote to a friend in London.

In Dublin, the Dáil approved the treaty by the majority that was bigger than the minority by only one vote. And, right away, the Irish independence movement was split into pro-Treaty and anti-Treaty groups. De Valera resigned as President of the Dáil because "the majority have no right to do wrong," and went around Ireland urging his followers to rise in a civil war against the British-approved Irish Free State. And so, the Irish Civil War broke out. IRA anti-Treaty forces occupied the Four Courts buildings in Dublin proclaiming them the headquarters of the Republican Government of all Ireland. Then, a British army general, the former commander of the British forces in Ireland, was assassinated by the IRA on his doorstep in London. Lloyd George called Collins (now Chairman of the Irish Free State Provisional Government) threatening to send British troops back to Ireland if Collins didn't put down the rebellion. Collins ordered the Free State army to bombard the IRA at the Four Courts. For that he borrowed cannons and ammunition from the British troops.

Bombardment of the Four Courts

Above: Free-staters ambush the IRA; Below: Free State General Seán Mac Eoin – left, IRA fighters – right

Churchill praised Collins, "If I refrain from congratulation, it is only because I do not wish to embarrass you," he wrote, and continued to provide arms and ammunition for Free State forces across Ireland. Collins became commander-in-chief of the Free State army.

The civil war lasted for 11 months, but early in the war the Free State army seized control of the big cities, while the IRA was more active in rural areas. The Free State Provisional Government was ruthless with its former comrades-in-arms. It ordered the execution of 3 anti-Treaty republican prisoners for every IRA attack. 77 men were executed – more than those put to death by the British authorities before the Treaty. In many areas republican prisoners were simply murdered right after capture. In Kerry 9 Republicans, who ambushed and shot some Free State soldiers, were tied to a landmine, and it was detonated.

In August of 1922 Michael Collins traveled to his native Cork county to visit Free State troops. Under the pretext of 'inspecting' his troops, he secretly reached out to the Republicans looking for a solution to the conflict. With a unit of pro-Treaty forces, he left Cork city, and, on his way to the countryside, stopped at a pub to ask for directions. The pub owner was an anti-Treaty IRA member. He recognized Collins and rushed to gather IRA locals for an ambush. They set up a roadblock on a turn in the road and waited in the hills that overlooked it. When Collins and his men were returning to Cork in the evening, following the same route, they spotted the roadblock, jumped out of their cars and prepared for combat. The gunfight followed. Collins was shot in the head. His last words were "Forgive them. Bury me in Glasnevin with the boys."

Collins' sister Hannie, who lived in London, mentioned to a couple acquaintances that she would be leaving for Ireland, to go to her brother's funeral. That day she received train and boat tickets paid by an anonymous 'friend.' That 'friend' was Winston Churchill. Years later Churchill wrote about Collins: "Michael Collins was a man of dauntless courage. He was an Irish patriot, true and fearless...We hunted him for his life, and he slipped half a dozen times through steel claws... He had those qualities of action and personality without which the foundations of Irish nationhood would not have been re-established."

Free State officers at Michael Collins' ambush site

The city of Cork during the war for independence

ATATÜRK
1881 – 1938

The Turkish Ottoman empire was at its height in the early 16th century. From Constantinople, Suleiman the Magnificent ruled an enormous stretch of territory that included the whole of North Africa. In 1529 his armies stood 'at the gates of Vienna' and it looked like Western Europe was about to fall under Turkish control. But the Austrians defeated Suleiman, and the slow, 350-year decline of the Ottoman Empire began. By the early 20th century it was bankrupt, impoverished, nicknamed the 'sick man of Europe,' and the vultures – Britain, Russia, and France – were circling over it snatching its pieces. Serbia, Bulgaria, and Greece broke away. France seized Tunisia, Britain grabbed Cyprus and Egypt... Germany sided with the Turks against other empires, but even the Germans knew – the Ottoman Empire was doomed.

The story of Kemal Atatürk is woven into Turkey's transformation from a collapsing empire into a young republic. The name Atatürk means "Father of the Turks." Kemal Atatürk received it from the Turkish parliament in 1934 in recognition of his role in establishing the Turkish Republic. Atatürk's birth name was Mustafa Efendi. He was born in the Turkish Quarter of Salonica – Thessaloniki in present-day Greece. His dad, Ali Riza Efendi, was a local customs officer whose family's lifestyle was very traditional, full of conventions and ceremonies tracing back to medieval times. For example, when Mustafa would enter the room where his dad was sitting, he would always kiss his father's hand and remain standing. Invited to sit down, he would say "I dare not sit in your presence." Then his dad would order him to sit down and the kid's response would be "I dare not disobey your command." Tradition also required that a male child be treated not as a kid, but more like a grownup, with ceremonial respect. The family was poor, because Mustafa's dad was honest and refused the bribes that made up most of the income of customs officials. Realizing that he might not have enough money to pay for his son's education, he quit his government job and started a timber business. When Mustafa was 9, his dad died and the boy went to work at his uncle's farm, cleaning stables and guarding sheep. Two years later Mustafa's mom, Zübeyde, convinced his uncle to hire her as a farm hand instead. She would work and save money to pay for Mustafa's education.

So 11-year-old Mustafa went to school. His classmates, however, didn't like him. They mocked him for his cheap clothes, and also for his blue eyes and blond hair – he didn't look Turkish at all. One day Mustafa beat up a kid who insulted him. The teacher punished Mustafa by flogging him with a stick. That day Mustafa walked out of the school and refused to go back there, even though Zübeyde cried and begged him to change his mind. Soon Mustafa asked their neighbor, an officer of the Turkish army, to help him enroll in a local military academy, and before his mom could stop him, he was a cadet. Mustafa was so good at math that his math teacher nicknamed him Mustafa **Kemal** – 'Mustafa the Excellent' in Turkish. At 17 Atatürk went on to a Senior Military School and then to a military college in Constantinople, the capital of the empire. His classmates described him as 'reserved,' silent, and mysterious.

As the Ottoman Empire drew closer and closer to collapse, many patriotic Turks dreamed of reforms and revolution. Atatürk and his friends read books that were prohibited in the empire – the works of the 18th-century French Enlightenment philosophers Voltaire and Rousseau and the writings of German and Russian revolutionaries.

Constantinople, late 19th century

Sultan Abdul Hamid II

They had to be careful. The Sultan, Abdul Hamid, had a wide spy network. Anyone reported to have liberal ideas was tossed in jail. In Constantinople Mustafa joined the Vatan ve Hürriyet ("Motherland and Liberty" in Turkish) – a secret society whose goal was to overthrow the sultan and establish a constitutional republic. One day a group of Vatan members, including Mustafa Kemal, got together at a cafe to interview a student who wanted to join their ranks. The student turned out to be a police agent. Atatürk and his friends were locked up in the rat-infested Red Prison. Nobody doubted that in no time they would be dead.

By that time Mustafa's mother, Zübeyde, had remarried. Her new husband was a wealthy merchant. Mustafa disapproved of the marriage and didn't talk to his mom. Later he reconciled with her and over the years his mom became the only person whose advice he would ever listen to. When the news of Mustafa's arrest reached Zübeyde, she rushed to Constantinople desperately looking for connections in the sultan's government.

She succeeded, and after a few weeks in prison, Atatürk was informed that because of his brilliance and youth the sultan had been gracious enough to pardon him. Atatürk was also told, "Be careful: You will not get a second chance." They put him on a boat leaving for Syria where he was to join a cavalry regiment stationed in Damascus. In Syria, Atatürk went right back to revolutionary activity. He was more careful now. For his caution and unbending spirit, his comrades nicknamed him 'Grey Wolf.' In 1907, at 26, Mustafa Kemal was promoted to the rank of Senior Captain and transferred back to Salonika where he joined the Committee of Union and Progress that led the *Young Turks* revolutionary movement.

Atatürk's mother, Zübeyde Hanım

A year later the Committee of Union and Progress staged a military revolt and a citizens' uprising that became known as The Young Turks Revolution. Deserted by the army, Sultan Abdul Hamid proclaimed a constitutional monarchy and invited the Young Turks' leaders to join his government.

Supporters of the Sultan, however, organized a counter-revolutionary military revolt, and even though the Young Turks managed to suppress it, Turkey plunged into political chaos. Using this opportunity, Austria annexed the Ottoman provinces of Bosnia and Herzegovina, Greece snatched the island of Crete, and Italy invaded the Ottoman province Tripolitania – present-day Libya. Between 1908 and the beginning of the First World War, Atatürk was sent from province to province – to Albania, to Libya, to Bulgaria – suppressing rebellions and defending Ottoman possessions from foreign invaders. Serving under the Young Turks' government, he despised them as traitors, believing they had sold themselves to Germany, on whose protection they relied. German support wasn't free, he thought, at some point Turkey would have to pay for it at the expense of its independence. Atatürk's own position was "Turkey for the Turks." The Young Turks were aware of it, so in 1913, at age 32, Atatürk was sent to Sofia, Bulgaria, as a military attaché (representative) to Balkan states (Southeast Europe).
It was, basically, an exile.

In Sophia Mustafa Kemal was invited to a New Year's Eve ball, where he spotted a beautiful girl and invited her to dance. Her name was Dimitrina Kovacheva. It was love at first sight.

Mustafa and Dimitrina got together – secretly – the next day and started dating. But she turned out to be the daughter of a Bulgarian general against whose forces Atatürk had fought only a year or so before! Atatürk asked Dimitrina's parents for her hand in marriage – twice, and was bluntly refused. His biographers say that this was a 'wound' that never healed.

When the first World War broke out in 1914, Turkey was an ally of Germany. Atatürk thought it was madness, but he was a soldier, and so he fought for Turkey and Germany, and gained enormous respect and authority in the Turkish army. He was now Mustafa Kemal Pasha – a general, but he shared the discomforts and dangers of his soldiers, winning their loyalty. When English shells whistled over the Turkish trenches, Mustafa Kemal sat calmly in the open smoking a cigarette and refused to take shelter. His soldiers believed that he was protected by divine providence.

Dimitrina Kovacheva; Turkish dagger, 18th century

"Gallipoli Campaign" (diorama at the Atatürk and War of Independence Museum, Istanbul)
World War I – Ottoman soldiers defending the Turkish Straights from the British forces in the Gallipoli Campaign. British expedition to take over the straits was launched by the head of British Admiralty, Winston Churchill. It failed, with 60 thousand dead on each side. Atatürk was one of the Ottoman commanders in the campaign.

In most campaigns Atatürk was forced to obey German commanders. He protested this, and in 1918 he was temporarily removed from the frontlines. His new job was to accompany the Ottoman crown prince Mehmed Vahideddin on a visit to Germany. On this trip Atatürk traveled to the Western Front and realized that German commanders had no strategy to win the war. When he asked German Marshal Ludendorff, who was planning a new offensive, what objective it was supposed to achieve, the answer was, "Will Your Excellency have a cigar, or do you prefer a cigarette?"

The Armenian Genocide

While Turkish armies fought on the frontlines, the Young Turks leaders decided to deal with an 'internal enemy' – the Armenian population of the Ottoman Empire. Defeats on the front weakened the government's authority across the country, and Armenians were expected to rebel and try to capture Eastern Turkey which, in ancient times, belonged to Armenian kingdoms. So the Young Turks started a systematic massacre of Turkey's Armenian minority, eventually killing around a million Armenians in the series of events that became known as the Armenian Genocide. In 1915 they started sending Armenians on 'death marches' – traveling on foot without food or water under the scorching sun – to the Syrian desert. The survivors of these marches were kept in concentration camps where they were gradually slaughtered.

Turkish soldiers, World War I

In 1918 the Ottoman Empire lost the war. Following the Armistice of Mudros, British, French, Italian, and Greek troops marched into Constantinople. Among the residents of the capital there were many liberal, pro-European Turks, ethnic minorities, and Europeans who welcomed the occupation. As the columns of French troops entered the busy multicultural Pera district, they saw the streets decorated with Allied flags and flower garlands. People cheered them from the balconies, "Vive la France! Vive la liberté!" (French for "Long live France! Long live liberty!") Wealthy Christian Arab and Greek families invited French officers to balls and parties. But when the occupation troops crossed the Golden Horn into the Old City, its streets were empty, all window shutters drawn, bazaars deserted.

Under foreign occupation, Mehmed Vahideddin became the sultan. Some Young Turks government leaders fled the country, others were captured and imprisoned in Malta. Constantinople was firmly in control of foreign troops. In Anatolia, however, the new nationalist movement was gathering strength and an anti-occupation revolt was brewing. Atatürk got in touch with patriotic Turks trying to organize resistance. He lived in a small house in the suburbs of Constantinople, aware that his every step was watched and recorded by government spies. He expected to be arrested any day. Instead, out of nowhere, he received the news that he had been appointed the Governor General of the Eastern provinces of Turkey and was ordered to suppress the nationalist rebellion in Anatolia! This gross miscalculation by the Ottoman government decided the fate of Turkey.

French troops enter Constantinople

In Anatolia, Atatürk brought other Turkish military commanders to his side. He told them he wasn't planning a revolt against the Sultan. He was saving the Sultan from the enemies in whose hands he was a prisoner. "Loyalty to Constantinople is treason to the nation," he said. The Sultan ordered Atatürk to return to Constantinople. The answer was, "I will stay in Anatolia until our nation has won its independence." So Atatürk was dismissed from the army. Next, Marshal Kiazim Karabekir, commander of the Turkish troops in Anatolia, received an order to arrest Atatürk. He called Atatürk to his headquarters and told him, "I've given my word to support you, but at the same time I am bound to obey the Sultan." "It's up to your Excellency whether we, Turks, are to be slaves or free men," responded Atatürk. Karabekir asked for a few minutes to think, then called Atatürk to his office. "Our sultan is a British puppet," he said and tore the sultan's order. Atatürk told his officers, "We'll have to face great risks and make great sacrifices. Once started, no one must desert, no one should look back or regret." The troops pledged loyalty to him on condition that the Sultan should not be harmed. Atatürk organized his movement into a political party and formed a shadow government in Ankara.

Meanwhile the Allied Western powers came up with a peace treaty – the Treaty of Sèvres – that partitioned (divided) the Ottoman Empire. France got Syria and Lebanon, Britain got Iraq and Palestine (present-day Israel and Jordan). The Ottoman provinces in the Arabian Peninsula went to Saudi Arabia and Yemen. The Persian Gulf provinces – Kuwait, Bahrain, Qatar and others – were divided between the Emirate of Riyadh (Saudi Arabia) and Britain. But most disturbing to patriotic Turks was the allied powers' intent to divide the territory of 'heartland' Turkey. Under the pretext of protecting the Christian population of the Ottoman Empire, most of Turkey was to be governed by 4 'Christian administrations' – Greek, French, Italian, and Armenian. Only a small portion of Central Turkey, cut off from the sea, was to remain the Turkish state. The sultan in Constantinople accepted the partition plan. Atatürk, in Ankara, rejected it. The Turkish Civil War began – between 'Kemalites,' the nationalist forces of Mustafa Kemal, and the Sultan's 'Caliph's Army' equipped and paid by the British. In addition to fighting the Sultan, Atatürk's National Army faced the Armenian forces in the East, and the Greek army in the West – also funded and armed by the Allied Western powers.

Things didn't look good for Turkish independence fighters. They were running out of weapons and ammunition. There was no money to pay soldiers, and their troops deserted in large numbers. The Greek army took Smyrna (Izmir) and was marching across Anatolia with little resistance. There was panic in Ankara. But, suddenly, help arrived – from an unexpected direction.

In 1917 the violent October Socialist Revolution shook Turkey's northern neighbor, Russia. The power in the country was seized by the socialist **Bolshevik** party led by Vladimir Lenin, and a bloody Russian Civil War between the Bolsheviks' revolutionary Red Army and

The Bolsheviks

*The Bolsheviks (from the Russian **bolshoi** = big and **bolshinstvo** = majority) were a far-left group of Russian revolutionaries led by Vladimir Lenin. After the victory of the October Revolution of 1917, the Bolshevik party was renamed the Communist Party of Russia.*

the counter-revolutionary White Army, followed. It was an empire collapse, similar to what was going on in Turkey. Russia exited the World War and made peace with the Germans. At that point Russia's former allies – Britain, France, Italy, Greece, the United States, and others – invaded Russia from every direction. Since Turkish nationalists were fighting the same Western powers, Russians wanted them to win. A steady stream of gold and weapons started flowing from Russia to Atatürk in 1920. All Anatolian men capable of fighting were recruited in the army. Women were also on the frontlines, unloading deliveries of ammunition and carrying artillery shells to Turkish firing positions. The 'Kemalites' began winning. The Armenian rebels fled to Russia-controlled Armenia. 60 thousand Turkish troops defeated a 200-thousand-strong Greek army on the Sakarya River, only 80 kilometers away

Below: British troops hold a parade in Constantinople in 1918;
Right: US troops hold a parade in Vladivostok, Russia, in 1918

from Ankara. Soon Atatürk's forces took Smyrna. In the port, thousands of Greek civilians and soldiers crowded on the boats leaving for Greece. Off the coast lay British warships. British officers watched the fighting and the chaos in the city. They received no order to assist the Greeks. Within weeks the Allied troops themselves started to withdraw from Constantinople. One and a half million Greeks were deported from Turkey – bearing only what they could carry.

Atatürk wanted his country to be a modern westernized republic, but the majority of Turkish leaders still preferred a constitutional monarchy, with the Sultan as its ruler. British journalist Grace Ellison in her book *An Englishwoman in Angora* (Ankara), wrote about Atatürk, "To me he seems like a professor, who must be forever explaining to his people what their nationalism really means." Atatürk waited for an opportunity to sway the Turkish public to his side, and it soon arrived. The Allied powers organized the Conference of Lausanne to 'rethink' the partition of the Ottoman Empire which couldn't be fully implemented after the victories of the nationalist forces. Instead of inviting the winning side, Atatürk, to represent Turkey, the British government invited Sultan Mehmed. The National Assembly in Ankara was beside itself with rage at such an insult, and Atatürk was able to push through a law abolishing the Sultanate. "Sovereignty is not passed on," he said addressing the National Assembly, "It is gained by conquest. Long ago the sultans of the House of Osman seized it. But today it's our nation that has secured it."

The Battle of Sakarya River (diorama at the Atatürk and War of Independence Museum, Istanbul)

Turkish army enters Izmir

Atatürk's troops entered Constantinople. The Sultan escaped from his palace in an ambulance and was evacuated by a British battleship. He died in exile, in Italy, in 1926. On October 29, 1923, Turkey became a republic. Atatürk was elected the President of Turkey and channeled all his efforts into turning his near-medieval country into a European-style power with a secular democratic government and modern economy.

Grace Ellison recalled her first meeting with Atatürk in Ankara: "The Pasha was wearing a big astrakhan hat and smoking cigarette after cigarette. His piercing, almost stern, glance reminds you that you will do well to say clearly and quietly what you have to say – and go! He has the face and the expression of a conqueror, but his voice is that of a cultured man of the world... his fair hair, well brushed back, his close-cropped mustache, his well-tailored clothes with the correct crease, would surely carry him through a London drawing-room without a guess that he was not English." In his home office there was "a large desk, some fine plants, and the usual Turkish or Persian rug...One of the two pianos in Angora stood in a corner. On the walls hang jeweled swords and other trophies sent by Muslim rulers to the conqueror they all acknowledge." Grace Ellison asked Atatürk if it was true that he was a fan of Napoleon. "Napoleon put ambition first," he replied. "He fought for himself, not for the cause." She noticed his mother's portrait on the wall and asked him if it was true that he admired his mom. "That's only natural," he said. "Oriental, if you will. The man whose hands are smeared in blood, whose soul is black with crime – even he bows in respect to his mother. You might as well be surprised that the sun shines."

Astrakhan Hat

The Astrakhan hat is made from karakul – the fur of the karakul breed of sheep. It became popular in Russia, Central Asia, India, and Turkey in the early 20th century. It was worn mostly in the cities by men of the professional class. Its name comes from the city of Astrakhan in the South of Russia.

When Ellison complimented Atatürk on his success, his response was, "I did my duty." "I have talked with many of Europe's great statesmen, but found none more modest than he," concluded Grace Ellison.

Atatürk introduced the metric system and switched Turkey from the Julian to the Gregorian calendar. European city planners and architects were brought in to modernize the cities. Mud swamps around Ankara were drained. Foreign goods were kept out of the country to promote the growth of local industry. Atatürk encouraged the visual arts, which had been suppressed under the Islamic laws of the Ottoman Empire. He opened museums and promoted sports. Book publishing, film, and a commercial music industry began to grow. In 1928 Turkey switched from Arabic script to the Roman alphabet. Thousands of secular (non-religious) schools were built in Turkey. "The greatest war is the war against ignorance," said Atatürk. He wrote a geometry textbook. Most of the math terminology used in Turkish schools today was translated into Turkish by Atatürk himself. He held parties and balls for his friends and insisted that all guests danced European style dances – whether they knew them or not! Women's education took off and soon there appeared female doctors, lawyers, and public officials. As a result of Atatürk's reforms, Turkish women became socially equal to men in their rights.

The Julian and Gregorian Calendars

The Julian calendar was introduced in Ancient Rome, in 46 BC, by Julius Caesar. It is a solar calendar of 365 days with a leap year (366 days) every four years (making the average year 365.25 days). The problem with the Julian calendar is that it gains one full day every 129 years, gradually undermining its accuracy. To improve the Julian Calendar system, scholars came up with the Gregorian calendar – in 1582, under Pope Gregory XIII. The Gregorian calendar reduced the average length of the year from 365.25 days to 365.2425 days. It's much more accurate in that it gains only 0.1 day over 400 years.

The Fez

*The biggest challenge for Atatürk was to make Turkish culture more European. One of his first steps in westernizing Turkey was his battle against the **fez** – the iconic Turkish men's felt hat with a tassel. Atatürk called it 'a sign of ignorance.' The name 'fez' comes from the Moroccan city of Fez, where they used berries to produce red dye. In the early 19th century Sultan Mahmud II ordered government officials to stop wearing the turban and switch to the more modern fez. But Atatürk now saw the fez as a symbol of the dead Ottoman Empire. He convinced the Assembly to forbid the wearing of the fez. Police were allowed to knock fez hats off the heads of those who kept wearing them. The Turks protested, but after a few hundred beatings, shootings, and executions, the fez was well and truly gone. Atatürk's government also banned the headscarf worn by many Muslim women.*

Atatürk didn't have kids of his own, but he adopted 9 orphans and paid for their education in boarding schools. Among them was the world's first female fighter pilot, Sabiha Gökçen. According to his adopted kids, Atatürk was a caring dad.

In 1922, when Atatürk entered Smyrna with the Turkish army, local supporters introduced him to Latife, the daughter of a Turkish shipping company owner. Latife was impressively educated. She had graduated from the Sorbonne University in Paris and also studied in London. Mustafa Kemal married her early in 1923 and she became the 'face' of a 'modern' Turkish woman – wearing European outfits instead of traditional Turkish Islamic women's clothing. But something didn't work out and two years later the couple divorced. Then Atatürk's mother died, and he started suffering from fits of depression. For a few years before his death he lived almost as a hermit, drinking half a bottle of raki (Turkish traditional alcoholic drink) and smoking three packs of cigarettes a day. He refused to see anyone except a few close friends with whom he occasionally played poker. He believed that the republic he had created didn't need his 'help' anymore. It had enough patriots and talented leaders. Once, over poker, Atatürk told the British ambassador, "When I die, there will be a thousand men to replace me." "Your Excellency exaggerates a thousand times," replied the Brit.

MAHATMA GANDHI
1869 – 1948

Mohandas Karamchand Gandhi was born into a well-to-do family. Both his grandfather and his dad were prime ministers of the small Indian princedom of Porbandar in Gujarat, the Western coast of India – under the British Raj, the colonial rule of the British Empire. Gandhi's family belonged to the Vaishya *caste*. Indian society was still nearly-medieval – divided into fixed social groups – 'castes' – to which people belonged by birth. The top caste in social prestige was the Brahmins – the Hindu priests and their families, the Kshatriya – warrior caste – made up much of the aristocracy and government workers, the Vaishya caste members were mostly merchants and farmers, and Shudra caste members were the working people. There were also the 'outcasts,' or *untouchables* – members of tribes 'outside' the caste system that were considered 'unclean.' They were not allowed to enter Hindu temples, use the same water supply or send their kids to the same schools as other Indians. They had to shout a warning when walking in the streets to make sure nobody accidentally touched them. Each of the castes was divided into hundreds of subgroups depending on a person's region of birth and racial characteristics. Many professions and careers depended entirely on a person's caste. All marriages were 'arranged' – agreed to by families of the same caste, based on the astrological 'compatibility' of bride and groom. The British colonial administration of India supported and strengthened the caste system (since it kept the Indians divided). Jobs in the British administration were available only for Indian Christians and members of the top castes. Many bizarre laws passed by the British deepened the social split of Indian society. For example, the Criminal Tribes Act of 1871 declared that people who belonged to certain castes (most Shudras and untouchables, as well as 'non-loyal' independence-seeking tribes in the North and South of India) were born with criminal tendencies. They were restricted in which regions of the country they were allowed to visit and who they could socialize with. The Colonial Land Alienation Act of 1900 proclaimed some castes and tribes not eligible to purchase and own land. This attitude of the British caused many educated young Indians to question how really 'civilized' the Western civilization was, and to reject 'westernization.'

Mohandas Gandhi's family were strict Hindus, following every bit of ancient customs and traditions. Gandhi's mom visited temples, said prayers and fasted on the many Hindu fast days. Once she gave a vow that she would fast during the rainy season, eating only when the sun emerged from the clouds. Her kids, including Mohandas, sat outside waiting for any glimpse of the sun and ran home to tell her when she could eat. Later Gandhi admitted that his family's worship practices left him cold, because he didn't understand the philosophical basis of Hinduism. Also, when it came to 'believing' in the divine origin of the castes, even as a kid Gandhi had doubts. One day, in the street, he deliberately touched an 'untouchable,' and, at home, intentionally didn't perform the ritual of 'purification' supposed to clean him from the contact with 'the unclean.' When he was 12, he realized that the British used the ancient caste system to keep large numbers of hard-working people poor and uneducated, and vowed to help the 'untouchables' rise from poverty and oppression. Gandhi also rebelled against other traditional beliefs, such as the Hindu prohibition on eating meat. With one of his classmates, who believed that meat gave Europeans colonial 'superiority,' he secretly purchased and cooked meat, and also smoked cigarettes. But eating meat or smoking didn't seem worth lying to his parents. "One thing took deep root in me," wrote Gandhi in his autobiography, "the conviction that morality is the basis of things, and that truth is the substance of all morality. Truth became my sole objective."

Jaipur, India, 19th century

When Gandhi was 13, his family arranged a marriage for him. His bride was a 14-year-old girl named Kasturbai. "As we didn't know much about marriage, for us it meant only wearing new clothes, eating sweets and playing with relatives," Gandhi recalled. Gandhi and Kasturbai each lived with their own parents until they moved in together a few years later. Soon Gandhi's dad died and the family faced financial hardships. When Gandhi was 18, a Brahmin priest advised him to go to London to study law, but his mom was against it. In London her son would be tempted to drink alcohol, smoke, eat meat, and flirt with girls, she thought. Gandhi, however, was desperate to go, so on his mom's request he gave an oath to do none of the things his mom suspected he would do.

In London, Gandhi first tried to embrace European culture. He bought himself a fancy suit and a violin, and started taking music and dance lessons, but his enthusiasm didn't last, plus he was running out of money. He also bought a stove and cooked his own meals because vegetarian meals were not common at restaurants and groceries. A friend introduced Gandhi to the Bible. He found the Old Testament boring, but loved the parables and sayings of Jesus. He especially loved these words from Jesus' *Sermon on the Mount*, "Love your enemies, bless them that curse you, do good to them that hate you, and pray for those that despise and persecute you." Discussing religions of the world with his friends, Gandhi recalled an old Hindu saying, "There is only one God, but there are many paths to Him."

Once Gandhi had his law degree, his brother found him a job in the British colony of Natal in South Africa where there was a large Indian community. Indians started arriving in South Africa in the 1860s as ***indentured*** workers raising crops at sugar, coffee, and cotton plantations. They had to work for 5 years, after which they were allowed to stay in South Africa or return to India. Their wages were only enough to buy one meal a day, yet some of them chose to starve and save enough money to open grocery shops and even small farms of their own.

Gandhi and Kasturbai

Indentured Worker

Indentured workers sign a debt agreement ('indenture') obligating them to work for their employers for a few years with no – or very small – wages in order to repay a loan or the expenses of emigration to a foreign country.

Gandhi with his coworkers in Johannesburg, 1909

When gold and diamonds were discovered in South Africa, thousands of Indians joined the gold and diamond 'rush' working in the mines. The British and Boer (Dutch) settlers didn't like the competition with the growing and successful Indian immigrant community. They passed laws that prohibited the Indians from owning land or houses, and banned them from traveling freely between British colonies.

In Natal, Gandhi was forced to feel like an 'untouchable.' In court he was ordered to take off his turban. In the street he was rudely pushed off the sidewalk – sidewalks were only for white people. On the train he was not allowed to travel in the 1st class compartment. On a horse-drawn coach he was told that only white passengers were allowed to sit inside. He had to sit outside, by the driver. European-owned hotels refused to serve him as a member of an 'underclass.' Some rude individuals called him a 'yellow man' and spit on him. Horrified, Gandhi told the owner of an Indian inn where he stayed about these humiliations. His host replied, "Only we, Indians, can live in a land like this, because, for making money we do not mind pocketing insults." These experiences further undermined Gandhi's faith in the 'civilizing' role of the British Empire.

South Africa, mid-20th century

In 1896 the government in the British colony of Natal proposed a bill banning its Indian and Chinese citizens from voting. Gandhi organized Indian business owners and professionals to submit a petition against the bill, and the bill was withdrawn. At this point, even though he had lost faith in European civilization, Gandhi believed that the only reason Indians were discriminated against in South Africa was because the British and the Boers were ignorant about the great Indian civilization. He thought of his own people as 'civilized,' 'white,' as opposed to Africans, and failed to see that Europeans' view of Indians was racially-prejudiced. Addressing his followers, Gandhi complained that the government was treating Indians 'at the level of kaffirs' (native black tribespeople). Defending voting rights for Indians, he wrote to the Natal government, "Anglo-Saxons and Indians come from the same Aryan stock, the Indo-European peoples." It took Gandhi years to realize that the colonial regime saw no difference between various 'colored' groups – be those Africans, or Indians, or the Chinese – they all were considered inferior.

After a vacation in India, Gandhi returned to Natal with his wife and 2 kids. When they arrived at the port of Durban, local European settlers organized a riot hoping to scare him into going back to India. Hundreds of men demanded his death. Gandhi was saved by the local police superintendent's wife who dressed him as a policeman and smuggled him out of the port. Colonial authorities detained the leaders of the riot and told Gandhi he was welcome to sue them in court, but he refused. "I have made it a rule not to go to court in regard to any personal grievance," he explained.

In 1899 the Second Boer War between the British Empire and the two Boer Republics began in South Africa. The Indians were uncertain whose side to take. Gandhi believed that justice was on the side of the Boers who fought for independence, but he called on the Indians to stand with the British. "Whatever little rights we have," he said, "we have because we are British subjects. If we desire to win our freedom, here is a golden opportunity to do so by helping the British in the war." He helped the Indians to form an Indian Ambulance Corps and received a war medal from the British government. Then the Zulu war broke out in 1906. "This was no war but a man-hunt," Gandhi recalled bitterly. He was given another medal for his service on the frontlines with the Indian Ambulance Corps that limited its work to helping the wounded Zulus. But the British government took Indians' loyalty for granted, and after the war, to Gandhi's disappointment, they refused to make Indians equal with white South Africans. More than that, the colonial governments continued to restrict

Leo Tolstoy

the rights of the Indian population. They adopted a new law requiring that all Indians should register with the government. All non-Christian marriages were declared illegal, which meant that Hindu and Muslim kids couldn't inherit their parents' property. The law was just a way to seize Indian businesses. Gandhi decided to fight against this new injustice with the method known as *Satyagraha* – "passive resistance," or *civil disobedience*. One of Gandhi's greatest inspirations in working out his own style of Satyagraha was the great Russian novelist and Christian philosopher Leo Tolstoy. Tolstoy believed that states and governments were violent by nature ("Robbers are far less dangerous than a well-organized government") and that citizens had a right to resist through non-violent disobedience. He criticized Christian churches for approving wars waged by national governments and taught that every Christian should be a *pacifist*. In 1908, Tolstoy wrote *A Letter to a Hindu* – an article where he suggested that India could gain independence through non-violent resistance. Gandhi read it and started corresponding with Tolstoy. In his autobiography Gandhi mentions Tolstoy's work *The Kingdom of God Is Within You* as the source of his original inspiration.

Pacifism

*Pacifism is the philosophy that rejects any justification for wars. It also rejects militarism, including military service and military industries. Both defensive wars and invasions are viewed by pacifists as criminal. The word 'pacifism' comes from the Latin **pax** – peace. A **peace sign** associated with pacifist movements combines the **semaphore** signals (signals used to send messages with hand-held flags) for the letters **N** and **D** – standing for 'nuclear disarmament.'*

Following Gandhi's call to resistance, Indian workers and business owners in Natal refused to register with the government. Their leaders were thrown in jail. Then Indian mine workers went on strike. The mine owners cut off their light and water supply. Then Gandhi led 6 thousand workers and their families to Transvaal, breaking the law that banned Indians from traveling between the colonies. But when they entered Transvaal, Gandhi was arrested and the workers were forced to return to the mines. While Gandhi was in jail, the Boer leader General Smuts sent him some books to read and reached out for an agreement. In return Gandhi knitted a pair of slippers for the general and they agreed that if Indians registered voluntarily, the government would repeal the unjust laws about marriage and property. Released from jail, Gandhi led more protests until the laws were finally repealed.

In 1915 Gandhi, his wife and two sons returned to India and Gandhi joined the Indian National Congress – a political party for India's national liberation. He started traveling around India organizing protests of Indian workers and farmers against unfair taxation and other colonial British laws. He also established his own *ashram* – a school of spiritual instruction and practice in Gujarat. Donations to the ashram supported his family.

Gandhi promoted extreme simplicity in one's daily life. He refused to employ servants or cooks. He, his wife and kids cooked their own food and did all the housework. "They were living on boiled rice and vegetables, together with whatever fruit was available in the local market," wrote Gandhi's supporter Acharya Kripalani in his book *Gandhi: His Life and Thought*. He also laughed at Gandhi as being "hopelessly unrealistic" because one of the rules at the ashram said, "If a man has too many buttons on his shirt or coat, it's equal to stealing." Things didn't go smoothly. Once a family of 'untouchables' came to the ashram and Gandhi admitted them. At once the stream of students and visitors stopped. Nobody wanted to share space with the untouchables. But there were powerful people around who supported Gandhi. As the ashram emptied out and the Gandhi family ran out of money, one day a stranger stopped his car at their door, silently put 13000 rupees in Gandhi's hand and drove away.

In the Champaran area of India's Bihar region, peasants were forced to grow indigo plants used to produce dye. But the demand for indigo dye fell and indigo farming brought very little money. Unable to win better terms from the local plantation owners, the Champran peasants came to Gandhi's ashram asking for help. He organized them in a protest against their employers and used his law expertise to improve their situation. "The most helpless and fearful groups of the Indian population rose, as if by a miracle, to cast off their fear and become conscious of their dignity as human beings," commented Acharya Kripalani. "It was in Champaran that Gandhiji came to be known as the *Mahatma*, the Great Soul."

During the First World War the British Empire received a lot of resources and support from India. In return, the British promised India self-government. Gandhi was hopeful that this would eventually bring India independence, so he appealed to Indians to join the British army and started touring the country with speeches, wearing a khaki recruiting sergeant's uniform. His efforts resulted in zero recruits. Everyone who knew him was puzzled at his naive faith in the British government's promises.

Many of Gandhi's supporters criticized him for conducting military recruiting activity, while preaching pacifism. After the war, in 1919, the British government broke its promises, and Indians rioted across the country. In Delhi police opened fire on a crowd of unarmed protestors. Gandhi fell ill and, for months, he couldn't regain strength. His doctor told him to quit the vegan lifestyle and at least include eggs and milk in his diet. Gandhi refused, but his wife, Kasturbai convinced him to start drinking goat milk.

One day Gandhi had a dream that prompted his next step. The whole of India should hold a day of fasting and prayer and embark on a movement of 'non-violent non-cooperation' with the British authorities. There is only one factor that enabled the British Empire to rule India for 200 years, Gandhi explained – Indian cooperation with the British out of respect for their industrial achievements and fear of their military might. The time had come to stop cooperating. Gandhi's non-violent protest actions were to include tax resistance, marches, boycotting English schools and British factory-made products, such as cloth manufactured in Britain. "Burn any British clothing you own," Gandhi asked. He wanted Indian villagers to start their own local manufacturing businesses and reject any European goods.

In 1920 Gandhi was arrested. In response, his supporters gathered in Amritsar, in the province of Punjab. The British military surrounded the crowd of protesters and opened fire on them. "Nearly 20,000 men, women and children had gathered in a square, walled in on all sides by multi-storeyed houses," recalled Kripalani. "It had only one narrow entrance. Hundreds of peaceful citizens, including women and children, were massacred. Hundreds more were injured and left to die without medical attendance or even water. Martial Law was imposed on the whole of the Punjab. What followed was a reign of terror. All our leaders were arrested and thrown into prison. Every effort was made to humiliate the protesters. In one street in Amritsar, they were compelled at the point of the bayonet to crawl on their bellies..."

Gandhi using a spinning wheel to spin thread

"...There was strict censorship of the press. No reports of the events in Punjab were allowed. But as days passed, rumors about the diabolical acts of the authorities spread throughout the country." Despite Gandhi's calls for non-violent resistance, chaos erupted and more blood was spilled: "Some demonstrators, who had been fired upon, became infuriated and chased a group of policemen into a police station. The station was burned down together with the policemen." (Kripalani) Muslims and Hindus started slaughtering each other. These events convinced Gandhi that what India needed wasn't self-rule within the British Empire, but full national sovereignty. He returned his war medals to the British authorities and wrote to the British Viceroy, "I can retain neither respect, nor affection for a government that has been moving from wrong to wrong in order to defend its immorality."

In 1922 Gandhi was arrested again, and sentenced to 6 years in jail for anti-government activity, but they released him 2 years later. Following another wave of Hindu-Muslim clashes, Gandhi called for peace and announced a 3-week fast as a symbolic payment for the sins of his people. The riots stopped.

Meanwhile Gandhi's non-violent non-cooperation and boycott movement grew, paralyzing the British administration. His resistance program included
- recognizing 'untouchables' as equal to other citizens
- cooperation between Hindus and Muslims
- demanding rights for women including abolition of arranged marriages
- prohibition of opium and alcohol
- expansion of the cotton thread spinning and weaving program to boycott sales of British-made cloth

Gandhi in London

Methods of civil disobedience

Civil disobedience is the refusal to comply with laws that are considered unjust. Methods of civil disobedience include
strike – *a refusal to work organized as a form of protest*
picketing – *the blockade of a workplace or a business, or a group of protesters blocking the entrance to a company building while calling on the public to not do business with it*
boycott – *refusal to do business or be a customer of a company or an organization*

In 1930 Gandhi led 78 volunteers in a 240-mile 25-day march from Ahmedabad to the village of Dandi, Gujarat, on the Arabian Sea coast. It was a protest against the British salt mining monopoly and salt tax. The plan was to break the salt monopoly laws by making salt from sea water. "Wherever they went, they received an adoring welcome by the people with flags and garlands," wrote Acharya Kripalani. "Gandhi spoke to the crowds at his prayer gatherings, morning and evening. As he marched on, the crowd of marchers swelled. Thousands joined him. Local administrations started crumbling. Nearly 400 village headmen resigned. Everywhere men and women were impatiently waiting to manufacture salt as soon as Gandhiji picked it up on the Dandi beach. The authorities who had ridiculed the movement now were scared. On April 6, early in the morning Gandhi marched to the shore where salt lay thick, and picked up the contraband salt and held it up in his hands for all to see. He remained in that area and carried on his work till he was arrested on the midnight of May 4. His arrest was the signal for a widespread strike. The cotton mills of Bombay and the railway workshops closed down. In Sholapur the workers defied the authorities who put the region under martial law. The British cruelly suppressed the workers, shooting 25 men... In Peshawar, batch after batch of non-violent protesters – men, women and children – marched forward to face the troops shooting at them. They bared their chests and challenged the authorities to do their worst. The shooting went on for hours, killing a large number of people. The Garhwal Battalion there ultimately refused to shoot at the unarmed people who were being brutally mowed down. As a consequence they had to face court martial, and many soldiers were sentenced to ten to fifteen years' imprisonment."

Salt March

The protesters who had marched with Gandhi approached a government salt depot in order to picket it. Native Indian policemen were sent to beat them up with *lathi* – metal-covered bamboo sticks. "They were beaten mercilessly but no one raised his hand even to ward off the blows. On the first day 320 were injured and two died." The salt protest campaign continued, and the British had to jail over 100 thousand Indians. Soon it became clear that changes were inevitable, and the British government promised to free all political prisoners if Gandhi and the Congress party called off the civil disobedience campaign. Gandhi agreed and started negotiations with the British, but the negotiations failed, and he was, again, imprisoned. Another round of negotiations took place in London in 1931...no agreement was reached, and, again, Gandhi called for a campaign of boycotts and ended up in jail. Despite his tense relationship with the British colonial leaders, Gandhi always pointed out that he didn't hate the British, just wanted to "part ways" with them. "Patriotism based on hatred kills," he said. "Only that based on love, gives life."

In 1942 Gandhi started the Quit India Movement. Its goal was to stop India's support for the British in World War II. Gandhi condemned Nazi Germany, but refused to fight for European democracies while India was denied a chance to be a sovereign state. The British responded with more arrests and over a thousand Indian activists were killed during the protests. This time Indian activists called for a violent response. After Gandhi was arrested, protesters burned down hundreds of railway stations and police buildings, and cut telegraph wires wherever they could.

In the mid-1940s the Indian political scene changed. The resistance movement was now split between the Hindu followers of Gandhi who demanded the British to 'Quit India,' and the Muslim League of India that asked the Brits to 'Divide and Quit India.' The Muslims wanted the partition of India into separate Hindu and Muslim states. Gandhi asked the Muslim League to cooperate with him in order to win independence for India as one nation. The decision on a partition could be taken later, through a *plebiscite* (all-citizens' direct vote), he suggested. But the Muslim community leaders rejected Gandhi's proposal. They called on Muslim activists to flood the streets in a protest they called "Direct Action Day," on August 16, 1946. In Calcutta the local authorities sided with the Muslims, so when Calcutta Muslims clashed with Hindus on Direct Action Day, the police weren't there to stop the violence. 5000 Hindus were killed and their property looted or burned. "The streets of Calcutta were covered with dead bodies that lay there for days. The manholes were choked with corpses." (Kripalani)

In response, Hindus started killing Muslims all across India. Thousands on both sides lost their lives. Gandhi fasted and begged both sides to stop the violence. When asked about these tragic events, he said, "We haven't lived and worked in vain all these years that we should become barbarians... I feel maybe it's just an indication that as we are throwing off the foreign yoke, all the dirt is coming now to the surface. When the Ganges river is flooding, the water is muddy. When the flood subsides, you see the clear blue water which soothes the eye. That is what I hope for and live for. I don't wish to live to see Indian humanity becoming barbarian."

The intensity of the protests and violence rose so high, that finally the British agreed to both grant India independence and to partition it into India and Pakistan. As the partition began, Muslims from India migrated to Pakistan, and non-Muslims – Hindus and Sikhs – traveled from Pakistan to India. In many areas these groups of refugees walked on the same roads in the opposite directions. In daily clashes over 500 thousand died. "As the biggest migration of population recorded in history was in progress, a most dangerous situation arose in the capital. Every fourth person in Delhi was a Hindu or Sikh refugee from Pakistan. They were furious not only against the Muslims who were at the root of the partition but also against the Congress party for agreeing to it." On January 30, 1948 a Hindu nationalist, who believed that Gandhi had betrayed India by allowing the partition, ambushed Gandhi on his way to a prayer meeting in Delhi. He fired at Gandhi at a close range and killed him. "It is well known that more than once Gandhi said that he could bring about Hindu-Muslim unity only by giving his life," wrote Kripalani. "And that is what unfortunately happened."

Left: A Hindu refugee camp in Delhi; Below: Muslim refugees climb on train roofs to leave for Pakistan

PATRICE LUMUMBA
1925 – 1961

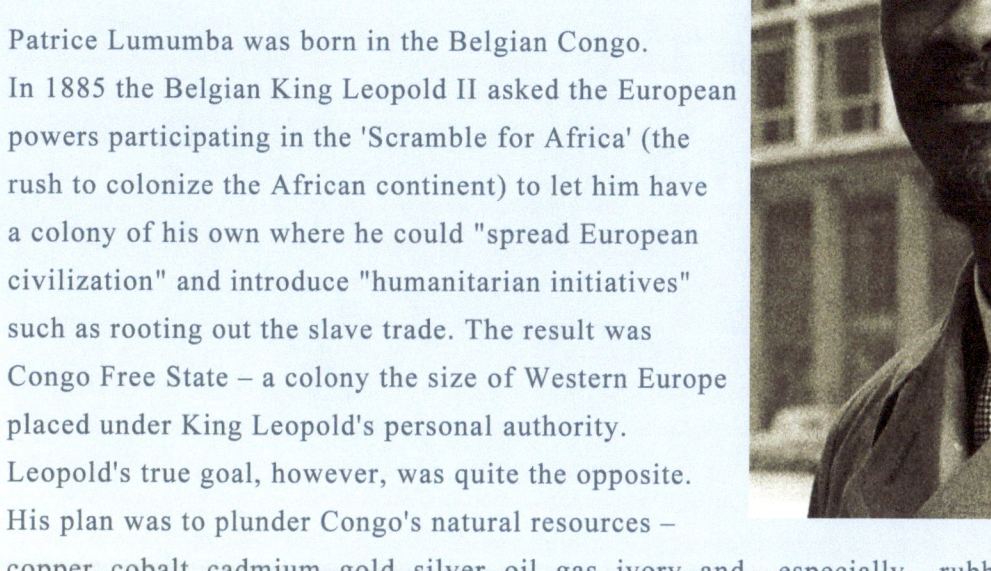

Patrice Lumumba was born in the Belgian Congo. In 1885 the Belgian King Leopold II asked the European powers participating in the 'Scramble for Africa' (the rush to colonize the African continent) to let him have a colony of his own where he could "spread European civilization" and introduce "humanitarian initiatives" such as rooting out the slave trade. The result was Congo Free State – a colony the size of Western Europe placed under King Leopold's personal authority. Leopold's true goal, however, was quite the opposite. His plan was to plunder Congo's natural resources – copper, cobalt, cadmium, gold, silver, oil, gas, ivory, and – especially – rubber. Rubber was hugely important for the European economy since the invention of the car – in those days all car tires were made of natural rubber.

European companies that got concessions to explore and extract Congo's natural resources forced native Africans into slave-like labor. Workers had to deliver daily quotas (specified amounts) of material, such as rubber, to their managers.

Rubber plants

Natural rubber is produced from latex – polymer particles in the juice of certain plants. Rubber plant growers make cuts in the bark of latex-producing trees and 'tap' the juice, collecting it into buckets. In Congo, the rubber plant grows as a small tree in the savannah or as a woody vine in the forests.

Below: Belgian Congo, 1958. Right: Rubber tree

If the quotas were not met, astonishing punishments would follow. For example, workers' hands were routinely cut off. After any instance of 'disobedience,' whole baskets of cut-off hands were brought to Belgian officials as proof that 'order' had been restored. Belgian officials also demanded that whenever a rebellious slave was killed, soldiers cut off the victim's hands to prove that bullets provided by the Belgians were not "wasted" on hunting. Torture and hideous brutality were the daily norm. Any resistance was suppressed by the Belgian army and native African mercenaries (soldiers-for-hire). Most mercenaries came from local tribes that practiced cannibalism – such as the Zappo Zaps, named so after the sound made by a rifle shot. The Belgians armed these Africans and sent them to raid villages that resisted forced labor. They encouraged the Zappo Zaps to massacre rebel tribes and terrorize survivors with 'cannibal feasts' in which thousands of people were cooked and eaten. The number of Congolese killed and those who died from overwork, torture, and disease during Leopold's reign is estimated at 5 to 8 million.

The brutality of King Leopold's regime caused outrage in Europe and the US. Among journalists and writers who published sharp criticism of King Leopold's colonial methods were Mark Twain and Arthur Conan Doyle.

Photos from Congo, 19th century

In 1908 Leopold was forced to sign a decree transferring the Congo Free State from his personal rule to that of his country, Belgium.

There was no school in Onalua, the village where Patrice Lumumba was born. So his dad sent him to the nearby Protestant mission school. At school, learning reading, writing, and arithmetic took about an hour a day. The rest of the day students learned working in the fields.
The missionaries were impressed by Patrice's thirst for knowledge and started giving him books to read at home. At 13 Lumumba went to a Catholic school where they had…palm oil lamps! Now it was possible to read all night long! Patrice loved books by the French Enlightenment philosophers Rousseau and Voltaire. He also started to write poetry.
He had perfect command of French and of two languages widely spoken in the Congo – Lingala and Swahili.

Concession = the right to use land or natural resources for commerce granted by a government to a company.

Chocolate Hands

Belgian chocolates in the shape of hands became popular in the 1930s. Supposedly the chocolate hands idea was inspired by a folktale about a young hero – the defender of Antwerp – who defeated an evil giant by chopping off his hand and throwing it into a river. However, by the 1930s the photos of Africans with missing hands had been seen by everybody in Belgium, and it's extremely unlikely that the chocolate manufacturers came up with their horrific 'chocolate hands' with no knowledge of the atrocities in Congo. Chocolate hands are still sold in Belgium today.

At age 18 Patrice Lumumba went to the nearest city – Kindu – to look for work. It was 1943 – the middle of World War II. Although the capital of the Belgian Congo was occupied by the Nazis, European mining companies in Katanga, a province in the south, kept exporting Congo's mineral resources to the US. One of these exports was uranium. The atomic bombs dropped by the United States on the Japanese cities of Hiroshima and Nagasaki used Congolese uranium. Patrice Lumumba first worked in one of the Katanga mining towns, and then moved to the town of Stanleyville where he found a job as a clerk at a railway company. Evenings and weekends he spent in the library.

In 1951, Patrice received a letter from his dad who informed him that a bride had been found for him and that marriage preparations were underway. The bride was an illiterate village girl, not the sort of partner Patrice had hoped for, but disobeying your parents was out of the question, so Patrice and his bride Pauline were married. They lived in Stanleyville, and Patrice became more and more active in public affairs. He started by organizing local discussion groups, progressed to political activism, and eventually became the leader of Congo's independence movement.

In 1952, Patrice Lumumba applied for a registration card, which was supposed to give *évolué* Africans equal rights with Europeans. The procedure was a humiliating test of the candidate's ability to 'live a civilized life.' You had to submit a lot of documents to a special commission and take various tests. Then commission members came to the évolué's home to see whether he and his family slept on European-style beds, used knives and forks, whether the husband beat his wife, and so on. Lumumba passed all the checks, but was denied the registration card due to "immaturity." His white friends, however – outraged – appealed to a Congolese court and Lumumba received the card.

Évolué

Évolué – from the French "evolved one"- was a label used by the French to refer to native people who became 'europeanized' through European-style education and the adoption of a European lifestyle. Évolués spoke French, dressed in European clothes, lived in the colonial cities, and held low-level office jobs.

In 1957 the French and British African colonial regimes started collapsing. The British Gold Coast became independent Ghana, the first de-colonized country in sub-Saharan Africa. French president Charles de Gaulle proposed a plan for gradual decolonization. The only French colony whose population rejected de Gaulle's plan was Guinea, which demanded immediate independence. "In reaction, and as a warning to other French-speaking territories," wrote The Washington Post, "the French pulled out of Guinea taking everything they could with them. They unscrewed light bulbs, removed plans for sewage pipelines, and even burned medicines rather than leave them to the Guineans." In 1958 Patrice Lumumba founded a political party – the National Movement of the Congo. It condemned *imperialism* of the Western powers, *tribalism* (loyalty to one's tribe, rather than the state), promoted *pan-Africanism* and demanded "immediate independence in the shortest possible time without any conditions or reservations."

Pan-Africanism

Pan-Africanism is a worldwide movement that seeks to unify native Africans across the African continent and the Africans who live in other parts of the world in their opposition to colonial practices and in an effort to bring development to Africa and preserve its native cultures.

In 1960, under tremendous pressure from the growing Congolese liberation movement, the Belgian government agreed to Congo's independence. In the parliamentary elections Lumumba's party won, and Patrice Lumumba

Imperialism

Imperialism is the practice of extending power over foreign nations through military invasions, puppet regimes, and economic domination.

became the Prime Minister of the new, independent Congo. At the official independence ceremony King Baudouin II of Belgium praised the Belgians who "brought civilization" to the Congo, and the "genius" of King Leopold II. "Don't be afraid to come to us. We will remain by your side and give you advice," concluded the king. The Congolese viewed his attitude as **patronizing** (condescending, not treating his audience as equals). Patrice Lumumba responded with an improvised speech, full of anger:

"Our wounds are too fresh and much too painful to be forgotten," he said. "We were forced to do backbreaking work for wages so small that we could hardly afford to buy food, to have a home, or to educate our kids. From morning to night we were subjected to mockery, insults and blows because we were 'negroes.' Our lands were seized in the name of 'laws' that allowed the strong to oppress the weak... Europeans lived in mansions, but for blacks there were only crumbling huts. We were not allowed in a cinema, a restaurant, or a store, if European customers were there... And how can we forget the mass executions, when so many of our brothers died under bullets, or the prison dungeons where those who refused to submit to injustice were locked?" Hearing Lumumba's speech, the Belgian king felt insulted and almost left the ceremony. Patrice Lumumba didn't play nice with the Europeans.

King Baudouin II with Congo's President Joseph Kasavubu and Prime Minister Patrice Lumumba, 1960.

Joseph Mobutu

Sadly, after only one week of independence Congo plunged into anarchy and chaos. Patrice Lumumba replaced all white officers in the army with Africans, and appointed new military commanders, including Joseph Desire Mobutu, a former Congolese soldier who had worked for the Belgian colonial government. The new commanders were inexperienced, and there were rumors that Mobutu was an agent of Belgian intelligence and the CIA! In addition, native African soldiers expected promotions and salary raises, but the country's treasury was empty. So military riots and attacks on Europeans began. After a few Belgians were killed, Belgium sent troops to Congo, and had them occupy all the major settlements. Next, the province of Katanga seceded. Katanga was the most industrially developed province, almost equal in area to France. The leader of the Katanga separatists said that Lumumba's party was "promoting communism." But the actual reasons for the secession were the bribes and promises of wealth coming from Belgian and British mining companies. They were afraid to lose access to Katanga's mineral resources and didn't spare funds to buy 'puppets' who would follow their orders. Most white residents of Congo fled to Katanga. Soon the Kasai province, where there were large diamond deposits, also seceded. Unable to stop European mining companies from tearing Congo apart, Lumumba appealed to the United Nations and flew to New York where he asked the UN for military assistance.

In New York, Patrice Lumumba realized that the problem wasn't just European mining companies. He faced a much more powerful enemy – the United States, interested in Congo's uranium. In desperation, Lumumba presented the UN with an ultimatum saying that if Belgian troops don't leave Congo, he "will be forced to ask for the intervention of the Soviet Union." That step by Patrice Lumumba was equal to signing his own death sentence. Russia, or the Soviet Union, was the rival of the United States in the so-called **Cold War**. Russians were not interested in Congo's diamonds or uranium. Occupying 1/6th of all dry land on Earth, Russia had more resources than it needed, but it viewed decolonized Africa as a market for its industrial products, especially the weapons it exported. Soviet leaders also hoped that the ideas of socialism would be attractive to African countries, and that they would support the *Eastern Bloc*.

The Cold War

The Cold War is a term that refers to the period between 1945 – the end of World War II – and 1991 – the collapse of the Soviet Union. That era was marked by political tension between the United States and the Soviet Union. The United States led the **Western Bloc** *of capitalist industrial powers. The allies of the Soviet Union, countries with socialist-style economies, formed the* **Eastern Bloc**.

Following Lumumba's ultimatum, Belgian troops left Congo, and the United Nations sent 11,500 'peacekeepers' to 'help' him. However, instead of working with Patrice Lumumba, the UN troops ended up protecting the mines of Katanga and Kasai from the Congolese government! So, Lumumba turned to Russia, and it quickly provided Congo with planes, trucks, weapons, food, and medicines, bypassing the UN. Soon, troops loyal to Lumumba launched a successful offensive against the separatists in Kasai.

Russian journalist Yury Zhukov who visited Patrice Lumumba in 1960 wrote that because the Congolese government was ineffective, Lumumba had to deal personally with both matters of state and individual citizens' requests and complaints. At the entrance of Lumumba's house Zhukov saw a crowd that included "a merchant seeking to obtain a trade permit, an official trying to be transferred to another city, and a teacher who was seeking a salary raise." The Russian guests were led through the back door into a "modest office with hardly any furniture." The conversation was constantly disrupted by phone calls. Suddenly a military man ran into Lumumba's office and reported that "a group of disguised Belgian officers had landed at the airport... Lumumba said goodbye warmly, quickly walked out into the street, got into a jeep packed with soldiers, and rushed off to the airport 'to catch the Belgian scoundrels.'"

Leopoldville was flooded with anti-Lumumba flyers. One of them read: "Meat has become expensive! Life has become expensive! It's all Lumumba's fault. He drove away the Europeans who financed us!" Another read, "Lumumba will sell your wives to the Russians!" The UN representative in Congo, Rajeshwar Dayal, recalled: "The administration of the country was completely paralyzed. There was not a single Congolese who was familiar with jurisprudence and could work in the courts. Most Belgian doctors left, and people in hospitals were treated by nurses. Schools were closed due to the departure of Belgian teachers. Belgian personnel abandoned airport control towers, and air travel became an extremely dangerous business. Famine began in some parts of the country."

Finally, a group of conspirators led by Joseph Mobutu came up with a plan to overthrow Lumumba. The group was *curated* (directed) by Lawrence Devlin, the CIA agent in Congo. Mobutu told Devlin that "if the United States will guarantee recognition of his government, he will carry out a coup." Devlin guaranteed Mobutu the support of the US government.

So Mobutu announced on the radio that the army had decided to "neutralize" the prime minister and parliament in order to "bring the country out of the deadlock" Lumumba was placed under house arrest. In 1975 the US Senate created a commission that investigated assassinations of foreign leaders by the CIA. Among the documents published by the commission was a telegram sent by Devlin from Congo: "The only solution is to remove Lumumba from the scene as quickly as possible." The commission concluded that "the plot to assassinate Lumumba was approved by President Eisenhower." The CIA chief, Allen Dulles, later quoted Eisenhower as having said that he wished Lumumba would "fall into a river full of crocodiles."

Devlin was given a budget of $100,000 to 'remove' Lumumba. A few days later, a member of the CIA's Clandestine Service, chemist Sidney Gottlieb, prepared a poison, the effect of which would present the symptoms of a deadly tropical disease. He arrived in Leopoldville with a passport in the name of Joseph Brown and introduced himself to Devlin as "Joe from Paris." According to Devlin's memoir, 'Joe' handed him a bag that contained a vial of poison, an antidote, syringes (to inject the poison into food or toothpaste), rubber gloves, and a gas mask, and said: "The details are up to you, but everything must be clean, not a trace leading to the US..." Devlin thought the poisoning plan was stupid, but he was afraid to argue with 'Joe,' so he decided to "delay the task as long as possible." The UN troops didn't allow anyone into Lumumba's residence, and Devlin pretended he couldn't find a way in. Finally, the CIA sent another senior officer to 'help' Devlin, Justin O'Donnell. O'Donnell brought to Congo two assassination 'experts.' One – code name QJ/WIN – was "a foreign citizen with a criminal background recruited in Europe." The other – code name WI/ROGUE – was "a stateless soldier of fortune, a forger and former bank robber." Before being sent to the Congo, WI/ROGUE underwent plastic surgery to conceal his identity. O'Donnell's plan was to break into Lumumba's residence and kidnap him. Both agents – QJ/WIN and WI/ROGUE – stayed at the same hotel in Leopoldville, but they didn't know each other. Seeking to create a team for Lumumba's assassination, WI/ROGUE tried to recruit QJ/WIN, unaware that they both worked for the CIA! WI/ROGUE offered QJ/WIN $300 a month plus bonuses for joining "the execution squad." But QJ/WIN rejected the offer and reported WI/ROGUE to the CIA!

In November, 1960, taking advantage of a tropical storm, Patrice Lumumba slipped past his guards and escaped, driving off in the direction of Stanleyville in the Eastern Province of

Congo where his supporters had organized a resistance against Mobutu. But, on the way there, Lumumba was captured by Mobutu's troops and imprisoned at a military camp. His supporters, however, raised an army that eventually took almost half of the territory of Congo. In panic Devlin wrote to CIA headquarters: "The present government may fall within days, which will inevitably lead to chaos and the return of Lumumba to power." Also, the newly elected US president John F. Kennedy liked Patrice Lumumba! Kennedy was about to be inaugurated on January 20, 1961. Lumumba's enemies were running out of time. So, a new assassination plot was laid. Lumumba was to be transported to Katanga province where his enemies promised the Americans that they would kill him.

Mobutu's security officers took Lumumba and two other prisoners to Katanga on a private plane. All along the way they kept beating Lumumba. The plane crew, consisting of four Europeans, tried to stop the beating, saying it was a threat to flight safety. Finally, unable to bear watching the torture, the pilots locked themselves in the cockpit and came out only after landing. Then, at night, Lumumba and the other prisoners were taken to the countryside where a firing squad stood ready – 8 soldiers and 9 policemen. Graves had already been dug. "You are going to kill us, aren't you?" Lumumba asked. "Yes," came the answer. The prisoners were offered time to pray. They refused and were executed. Patrice Lumumba was 35 when he died.

As rumor of Lumumba's death spread around the world, Belgians and Mobutu's government tried to hide the crime. Lumumba's body was dug up from the grave, cut into pieces with a saw, and placed in a barrel of sulfuric acid. This task was performed by Belgian police officers. To keep themselves 'motivated,' the Belgians drank a lot of whiskey and, being drunk, spilled the acid needed to destroy Lumumba's body. So they buried his skull and bones in the jungle and took some of his teeth as 'souvenirs.' In 2001 Belgium accepted 'moral responsibility' for the death of Lumumba, and returned one of his teeth to his family in Congo.

Patrice Lumumba being taken to Katanga

FIDEL CASTRO
1926 – 2016

Fidel Castro's dad was an immigrant from Spain who became wealthy running a sugar plantation in Cuba. Fidel had 6 brothers and sisters. Even as a kid Fidel had a phenomenal memory. Although he wasn't enthusiastic about going to school, he was the best student in his class. His favorite subject was science. Observing the hopeless poverty of plantation workers, Fidel became interested in the ideas of social equality and socialist revolution. As a boy of only 13, he led the sugar cane cutters on his dad's own plantation in negotiating with the managers for better pay. In 1941 Fidel graduated from school with honors. According to his classmates, he loved baseball, was easily upset, and often participated in fights. Fidel studied law at the University of Havana, and having received his degree, he opened a private law practice – defending the poor in court. In 1948 Fidel married Mirta Díaz-Balart, the daughter of a wealthy Cuban politician. Mirta's dad gave the newlyweds a present – a three-month vacation in New York City!

In the early 1950s, a former Cuban president named Fulgencio Batista seized power in a military coup. Batista was supported by the United States. He banned Cuban trade unions and arrested members of Cuban socialist groups. Fidel Castro tried to fight Batista's government in court, but Batista ruled 'above the law,' as a dictator, so Castro and other members of the opposition started preparing an uprising. Its first battle was supposed to be an attack on the government military garrison at the Moncada Barracks near Santiago de Cuba. Fidel's fighters, wearing government military uniforms, were planning to capture weapons and ammunition of the garrison, and then recruit rebel fighters from among poor cane cutters on nearby plantations. The attack was carried out in 1953. It failed.

Fulgencio Batista

Many of Castro's men were killed by machine-gun fire. Out of those captured, 22 were tortured and executed without trial. Castro was lucky to survive and receive a sentence of 15 years in jail. At his trial Fidel Castro delivered his famous speech ending with the words: "History will absolve me." He also acted as a defense attorney for the rebels and convinced the judges that the charges of "organizing an armed uprising against the Constitutional State" were invalid because Batista's rule was a dictatorship, not a constitutional state. As a result, most of the rebels were acquitted!

Two years later Fidel Castro was released under an amnesty, but while he was in jail, his wife Mirta divorced him. Her uncle was Batista's Minister of the Interior, her whole family supported Batista, plus, while Fidel was away, she found some love letters he received. They seemed to indicate that Fidel hadn't been faithful to her. Out of jail, Fidel traveled to Mexico, where he organized the revolutionary "26 July Movement" (the date of the rebellion against Batista), or M-26-7. Fidel's fighters were known as **Los Barbudos** ("the bearded ones"). His own nickname was "El Comandante" (the Commander), and his right-hand man was the famous Argentinian revolutionary Ernesto Che Guevara. In 1955 Fidel visited New York where he opened an office and raised funds for a new uprising from the New York Cuban community who were opposed to Batista.

Right: Fidel and his fighters; Below: Che Guevara

In 1956 Fidel purchased an old beat-up yacht, Granma, and sailed from Mexico to Cuba. Designed for 9 passengers, the yacht carried 82 fighters, 2 grenade launchers, 90 rifles, 3 machine guns, and boxes upon boxes of ammunition. At the Cuban shore, the yacht ran aground. Fidel Castro and his men fled inland, but Batista's forces were hunting them. Out of 81 only 19 made it, with 2 automatic rifles. They set up a camp and started attacking local Batista garrisons in order to capture some weapons. Meanwhile, all across Cuba, anti-Batista revolutionaries organized riots and sabotage. Batista's government responded with mass arrests, torture, and secret executions. The news of these brutalities reached the US, and anti-Batista protests erupted there as well. As a result, the United States government, which had been supporting Batista, was forced to stop supplying him with weapons. That put an end to Batista's 'puppet regime.'

Only a few months after the arrival of the Granma in Cuba, Fidel Castro's rebels reached Havana and seized power. Massive cheering crowds greeted 32-year-old Fidel in the streets of Havana. He was now an international celebrity and the Prime Minister of Cuba. Within days of the victory, the Cuban rebel army executed over 200 Batista officers convicted of torture. Thousands more trials and executions of Batista supporters were carried out in the following months. The Cuban constitution prohibited capital punishment, but, since Batista's government ignored that, the rebels chose to ignore it too.

The Cuban state was to be reinvented from scratch. Fidel Castro's state-building program was based on the ideas of socialist revolution. It proposed a transition to the socialist economy – the transfer of land from plantation owners to peasants, *nationalization* (government takeover) of industry,

Above: A photo taken while Fidel's men were disembarking from the Granma in Cuba;
Left: Havana greets Fidel Castro

and free education. 200,000 peasants received land. Landowners were furious, including Fidel Castro's own mom whose land was distributed among her plantation workers. All businesses that belonged to foreigners, including US citizens, were nationalized. Thousands of wealthy and middle-class Cubans fled from Cuba to the US, as their property was seized by the revolutionary government.

These socialist policies caused a bitter split between the United States and Cuba, so Fidel Castro turned to the Soviet Union. The Russians sent oil, fertilizers, machinery, cars, industrial goods, food, and medicines to Cuba. Cuba paid Russia with sugar, fruit, and leather. Cuban oil refineries (plants producing oil products, such as gasoline, from raw oil), run by the US companies, refused to process oil imported from Russia. Fidel Castro responded by nationalizing them all. US president Dwight Eisenhower authorized the CIA to assassinate Fidel Castro and overthrow his regime. He also issued an economic *embargo* on Cuba and stopped the import of Cuban sugar. In response Castro nationalized US-owned banks and sugar mills.

Embargo and sanctions

An embargo is a ban on trade with a particular country. Sanctions are means of economic pressure that can include limiting or stopping trade with a particular country, or prohibiting economic aid to it. Sanctions can also be applied to companies and individuals.

In 1961 the US cut diplomatic relations with Cuba and started working toward the overthrow of the Cuban revolutionary government. The CIA paid for the military training of Cuban refugees and organized them into sabotage units. These units attacked ships delivering goods to Cuba, and blew up Cuban plants and sugar mills inside Cuba. The CIA also trained a 1,500-strong landing force to mount an invasion of Cuba. In April of 1961 American planes bombed Cuban military airfields, but the US government refused to accept responsibility for the attack and stated that the pilots were Cuban air force officers who had defected (switched sides). Fidel Castro responded by arresting up to 100,000 Cuban citizens suspected of sympathizing with the US. Finally, on April 17, 1961 the CIA-trained invasion force landed on the southern coast of Cuba, in the Bay of Pigs. But the Cuban refugees couldn't compete in military skills and motivation with the Cuban army led by Fidel himself. Only 3 days later the invaders surrendered. Over a thousand CIA-trained Cubans were interrogated on live TV and then deported to the United States in exchange for food and medicines.

The Bay of Pigs invasion pushed Fidel Castro and his government even closer to the Soviet Union. Cuba became a Soviet-style one-party state where citizens had no freedom of speech and were not allowed to leave the island. Religion was frowned upon. Most churches were shut down. On the positive side, Soviet engineers, teachers, and doctors arrived in Cuba. They founded schools, professional training centers, built plants, power stations, ship yards, bridges, roads, hospitals, cultural centers, and theaters. Thousands of young Cubans graduated from universities in Russia and returned to work in Cuba. In no time literacy in Cuba rose to 98%, medical care and education became free, child mortality fell below the level of European countries, and unemployment nearly disappeared.

Despite all this, the Cuban economy was not doing well. One day, soon after the victory of the Cuban Revolution, Fidel gathered his inner circle and asked them "Are there any economists here?" Revolutionary guerilla Che Guevara misheard the question. Thinking Fidel was asking if there were any 'communists' in the room, he raised his hand and was instantly put in charge of the Cuban economy as the head of the Central Bank and the Minister of Industries. Guevara was a poet, a doctor, and a fighter, with zero understanding of economics. Guevara despised finances so deeply that his signature, printed on Cuban currency bills, read simply 'Che' – the nickname he received because he often used the word 'che' – a filler word in Argentinian Spanish. It's similar to 'so' or 'well' while its original meaning is a 'guy,' a 'fellow.'

The Cuban socialist economy often suffered break-downs aggravated by the fact that Cuba depended so heavily on Russian aid. One day Havana's grocery stores were overflowing with Russian food and wines, and all gas stations worked. A week later there were shortages of food, medicine, gas... People grew disillusioned with socialism, but few dared to speak up. The dreaded Soviet military intelligence, the KGB, had trained the Cuban intelligence service – the G2 – which kept itself busy tracking down anyone suspected of counter-revolutionary activity. Over 14,000 people were executed during the decades that followed the Cuban Revolution. Two million Cubans fled the island – risking their lives. Many of them reported having been tortured.

Meanwhile, in the US, the CIA developed plan after plan to assassinate Fidel Castro. They tried to kill Castro while he was fishing, tried to shoot him with a miniature pistol built into a reporter's camera, tried to poison his cigars or fill them with explosives.

Nothing worked... Over the course of his life, Castro survived over 600 assassination attempts. The CIA assassination plots included poisoning Castro's diving suit with a fungus, poisoning his shaving cream with botulinum toxin, and rigging seashells on his favorite beach with explosive devices to be remotely detonated from a US submarine! One CIA agent arrived in Cuba with a pen containing a vial of poison and a needle in its tip, but the operation was canceled due to... the assassination of US President Kennedy! Twice CIA agents recruited people close to Castro. One of them was Fidel Castro's girlfriend Marita Lorenz who was jealous of him (not without reasons...). She was given poison pills, which she was supposed to drop in Castro's drink. However, the G2 had found out about this plot and, when Marita came to see Fidel, he handed her his gun with the words: "You want to try? Go ahead." She cried and confessed.

Some CIA operations targeted Fidel Castro's reputation – these were attempts to embarrass him publicly. One such plan was to strip Fidel Castro of his famous beard by spraying toxic thallium salt on his shoes while he stayed at a hotel on a visit abroad... Thallium would have made the hair of his beard fall out. The plot failed because Fidel canceled his foreign trip. Another failed plan was to spray an LSD drug aerosol at a television studio where Castro was to make one of his multi-hour speeches on live TV. CIA agents hoped that under the influence of drugs Castro would start hallucinating and appear insane. But something went wrong – again. In 2007 US President George Bush was asked at a press conference whether he thought the era of socialism in Cuba would one day be over. "One day the good Lord will take Fidel Castro away," answered Bush. The same day the 80-year-old Castro held a press conference where he was asked how he had managed to survive all the CIA assassination attempts. "Apparently the good Lord has protected me all these years," joked Castro.

Fidel Castro assassination-attempt authorizations by US presidents

(the actual number of assassination attempts was higher): Eisenhower – 38; Kennedy – 42; Johnson – 72; Nixon – 184; Reagan – 197; Bush (Senior) – 16; Bill Clinton – 21

Censorship paralyzed Cuban media, but there was one outlet that even the Cuban G2 couldn't suppress – the all-surviving Cuban humor. Thousands of jokes about Fidel Castro and his socialist economy circulated around Cuba and in the Cuban immigrant communities in New York and Miami. Fidel himself was reported to laugh uproariously at some of these jokes. Here are a few examples.

1. Fidel Castro is making a speech. "Look at all the poverty in America!" he says. "In Havana everyone has an apartment, but in Miami there are people sleeping on park benches!" The next day a classified ad appears in a Havana newspaper: "Will trade a two-bedroom apartment in Havana for a park bench in Miami."

2. A drunk Cuban tells his buddy, "I know who is to blame for the fact that there is no food and no gasoline." The buddy reports him, and he is grabbed by G2 agents. They interrogate him, "So, who is to blame?" "US President Bush, of course, who else?" responds the drunk. They let him go, and as he leaves the G2 office, he turns around and points at the G2 agents, "But I know who you guys think is to blame!"

3. Fidel Castro dies and goes to Hell. He can go to Capitalist Hell or to Socialist Hell. He first goes to Capitalist Hell. "What is it like here?" he asks. "We cut you into pieces and boil you in oil," replies the Devil. Terrified Fidel runs to Socialist Hell. At the gates of Socialist Hell there is a huge line of people waiting to get in. He eventually enters and asks the Devil what it's like in Socialist Hell. "We cut you into pieces and boil you in oil," replies the Devil. Fidel is indignant: "But... but that's the same as in Capitalist Hell! Why such a long line?" "Because sometimes we're out of oil, and sometimes we don't have knives..." sighs the Devil.

In 1962, Soviet leader Nikita Khrushchiov convinced Fidel Castro to allow Russians to station their nuclear weapons in Cuba. The result of this was the so-called Cuban Missile Crisis. When the US government discovered Russian nukes in Cuba, negotiations followed. Russians agreed to remove the missiles in exchange for a US promise not to invade Cuba and to remove American nuclear missiles from Turkey and Italy. In late 1991 the Soviet Union fell apart. The Russian Federation that emerged as its heir dropped socialism in favor of a free-market economy and stopped supporting foreign countries with socialist governments. This left Cuba in a deep economic crisis. The Cuban government was forced to bring back some freedoms and abandon many socialist policies. People were allowed to leave Cuba, to start and run private businesses, to accept foreign currency, and so on.

Fidel Castro remained the leader of Cuba until 2008 when he retired because of illness. He died in 2016.

www.ingramcontent.com/pod-product-compliance
Lightning Source LLC
LaVergne TN
LVHW071657060526
838201LV00037B/368